BiRDS
OF A
KiND

Also by Wajdi Mouawad
and translated by Linda Gaboriau

A Bomb in the Heart
Forests
Heavens
Scorched
Tideline (translated by Shelley Tepperman)

BiRDS

OF A

KiND

BY WAJDI MOUAWAD
TRANSLATED BY LINDA GABORIAU

Playwrights Canada Press
Toronto

For professional or amateur production rights, please contact:
Simard Agence Artistique
624 Ch Thomas-Maher, Lac St-Joseph, Québec G3N 0B2
514-578-5264 :: info@agencesimard.com

LIBRARY AND ARCHIVES CANADA CATALOGUING IN PUBLICATION
Title: Birds of a kind / by Wajdi Mouawad ; translated by Linda Gaboriau.
Other titles: Tous des oiseaux. English
Names: Mouawad, Wajdi, author. | Gaboriau, Linda, translator.
Description: First English edition. | A play. | Translation of: Tous des oiseaux.
Identifiers: Canadiana (print) 2019008250X | Canadiana (ebook)
20190089474 | ISBN 9781770919907 (softcover) | ISBN 9780369100658 (PDF)
| ISBN 9780369100665 (EPUB) | ISBN 9780369100672 (Kindle)
Classification: LCC PS8576.O87 T6813 2019 | DDC C842/.54—dc23

Playwrights Canada Press acknowledges that we operate on land, which, for
thousands of years, has been the traditional territories of the Mississaugas
of the Credit First Nation, Huron-Wendat, Anishinaabe, Métis, and
Haudenosaunee peoples. Today, this meeting place is home to many
Indigenous peoples from across Turtle Island and we are grateful to have
the opportunity to work and play here.

We acknowledge the financial support of the Canada Council for the
Arts—which last year invested $153 million to bring the arts to Canadians
throughout the country—the Ontario Arts Council (OAC), Ontario Creates,
and the Government of Canada for our publishing activities.

 Canada Council for the Arts   Conseil des arts du Canada   ONTARIO ARTS COUNCIL CONSEIL DES ARTS DE L'ONTARIO
an Ontario government agency
un organisme du gouvernement de l'Ontario

 Canada    ONTARIO CREATES | ONTARIO CRÉATIF

For Charlotte Esther Farcet
and this exhilarating fourth step,
the t moment of the Big Bang.

Birds of a Kind was first produced in English by the Stratford Festival at the Studio Theatre in Stratford, Ontario, on August 15, 2019, with the following cast and creative team:

Eitan: Jakob Ehman
Leah: Deb Filler
David: Alon Nashman
Etgar: Harry Nelken
Norah: Sarah Orenstein
Wahida: Baraka Rahmani
Eden: Hannah Miller
Doctor: Miranda Calderon
Waiter: Danny Ghantous
Rabbi: Ron Kennell
Nurse: Oksana Sirju
Wazzan: Aladeen Tawfeek

Director: Antoni Cimolino
Designer: Francesca Callow
Lighting Designer: Michael Walton
Projection Designer: Jamie Nesbitt
Composer: Levon Ichkhanian
Sound Designer: Adam Harendorf
Dramaturge: Bob White
Intimacy Coach: Anita Nittoly
Assisstant Director: Peter Pasyk
Stage Manager: Alison Peddie
Assisstant Stage Managers: Alice Ferreyra and Ann Stuart
Production Stage Managers: Marie Fewer-Muncic, Kim Lott, and Maxwell T. Wilson

CREON. An enemy, even after his death,
never becomes a friend.

ANTIGONE. I am made to love, not to hate.

—Sophocles, *Antigone*

Dramatis Personae

Eitan
Wahida
Eden
Leah
Norah
Etgar
David
Wazzan

nurse, waiter, rabbi,
doctor, nurse's aides, male nurses, employee

I
BIRD OF BEAUTY

1. The impeccable harmony of chance

Central hall of the library in a university on the East Coast of the United States. Varnished wood tables. People of all ages. Many with computers and earphones. A young woman is working at one of the tables, engrossed in an old book. A young man passes her, stops short, turns back and grabs the book away from her. She stands up, stunned. The young man examines the book, mesmerized. He looks at her, realizes what he just did and passes the book back to her.

EITAN. Excuse me.

The young woman takes the book and sits down. The young man leaves. Beat. The young man returns.

Sorry to bother you . . .

She removes her earphones.

You're probably going to think I'm crazy, but I've been trying to track you down for two years, without knowing who you are, how many you are or what you look like. Let me explain. You see, aside from the fact that this is my university campus, I always come to work in this library, even though New York has many others, just as grand, I never go anywhere else because of a strange coincidence that has been going on for two years. You won't believe me. But I'll tell you. Should I tell you? Let me tell you. Every time I've come here, to this immense library, in this immense university, in this immense city, I've always found this book on the tables where I sat down by chance and I never, ever met the person who borrowed it.

He picks up the book.

Ibn Khallikan's Biographical Dictionary, Wafayāt al-a'yān. I'm not sure I'm pronouncing that right. Please don't think I'm superstitious. I'm not superstitious and never once over the past two years did I try to read into the reoccurrence of this extraordinary coincidence a cabbalistic sign or anything like that, but it started to seem crazy. There are a lot of books in this university library, a lot of tables, maybe fifty, and each one can seat twelve people which can mean as many as six hundred individuals on some days. If every individual consults three books and dutifully listens to Mr. Wayne Jon Jackson who's constantly reminding us not to put the books back on the shelves ourselves, to let the staff do it, that can mean close to two thousand books left on the tables. And this book, *Wafayāt al-a'yān,* translated into English by William

MacGuckin and printed in Paris in 1843, is the only copy the university possesses. So it's not only the same title I find, by chance, on the table where I choose to sit, by chance. It's the same book. The same object. Do you understand? The probability of finding the same title is slim enough, but when you consider that I never sit at the same table, never on the same days and that I come at all hours, the fact that of the 634 times I came here, I found the same object 592 times is pretty wild, right? All probabilities are possible, you say, that's true, but some are rarer than others, and the rarer they are, the more beautiful. The impeccable harmony of chance, as Naji Abou Hamra, my statistics professor, always says. But one element needed clarification: was this book left by different people every time or was it always the same person? The first hypothesis leads us to the world of lovely coincidences, while the second leads to the world of grand harmonies, and if you were to turn out to be that person, I would have to question my view of the world. I'm the skeptical type who doesn't believe in anything. I'm not even a nihilist or a pure materialist, let's say I'm an *objectist* who believes everything is an object and who doesn't waste time indulging in idle daydreaming. I don't believe in signs. I don't believe in magic or the mysterious meaning of life. But the minute I saw you with that book, everything started to tremble, and I think I've lost control of my claustrum, my putamen and my anterior cingulate cortex, the parts of the normally constituted brain that are indispensable for the production of fantasies. But all the fantasies my brain might produce don't hold a candle to what I felt when you finally appeared after these two long years. To make myself clear: if the impeccable harmony of coincidence is you, then I'll have to renounce my convictions and start believing in horoscopes, in the invisible, in angels and the extraterrestrials who supposedly fabricated us in their laboratories, and I'll act like those simple-minded people who insist upon seeing in these chance moments, signs of fate, the hand of God and other such nonsense.

WAHIDA. And of course, you are not simple-minded.

EITAN. Not at all. I repeat: I'm not the type who attributes meaning to a mere probability. So there must be a scientific explanation.

WAHIDA. That would prove what?

EITAN. That our meeting is not due to chance.

WAHIDA. What might it be due to, then?

EITAN. To the Big Bang.

WAHIDA. Of course. How silly of me . . .

EITAN. Don't laugh, I'm serious. I can't see any other explanation. Up until the *t* moment of the Big Bang, in the time span that has neither beginning nor end, our matter, yours and mine, was already entwined with that of this book in a particle infinitely smaller than the head of a pin. Entwined to such an inconceivable extent that it took the Big Bang to separate us and 13.8 billion years for us to meet again in this library, you and me and the book, and to experience beyond time and space the initial sensation of connection. Well, so much for that. I hope you don't think I'm trying to pick you up.

WAHIDA. Never crossed my mind, but speaking of the Big Bang, in Harlem at the corner of 122nd and Lenox, they just opened a bakery / night club. It's called This is the End. The music is awesome and the donuts are to die for . . . Then you said something about the speed of light and the arc of time but I couldn't hear a thing, my heart was beating so loud in my ears. We stood up. You knocked over your chair. Mr. Wayne Jon Jackson got mad and we left, laughing. I'd forgotten how to walk, I couldn't believe what was happening. What a gift. At least I will have felt that once in my life. It's overwhelming, Eitan, a heart bursting. You and me. How could it possibly be mere chance? What determines a meeting? A book, a donut, a genocide three-quarters of a century ago. And what if this and what if that and if and if and if and if and if and if and if and if you and I hadn't met. Then the Big Bang would have led to nothing. Is that even possible, Eitan? The universe splits with every *if*. How many times have you told me that? We forget that in this very moment there exists a world in which you and I never met. If that's true, then I don't know who is unhappier, between me and me. Sorrow waits patiently in the wings. Its time has come. But I'd rather be a stone than that woman to whom you mean nothing. We walked down the wide steps of the library that day in the freezing cold of winter that was a pretext for holding on to each other. A joyful drifting. Forgetting everything else, our studies, New York, the rest of the world, simply a backdrop. We weren't asking for anything and everything was given to us. Life's treasure. The fusion when, making love, I felt you tremble, on the verge of tears, and I asked, Eitan, Eitan, what's the matter, what's wrong, and you: nothing, my love, it's magic for the man who didn't believe in magic. And now? Where is that magic? I've opened the window in your room. The night is so mild, the air so pure, everything feels like it was before, but what's the point, if you don't wake up? Eitan . . . I don't know how to notify your parents. I went to see that woman . . . Mrs. Kimhi, your grandmother, I told her, Eitan was one of the victims of the attack. She slammed the door in my face. What is going on? Eitan! Come back. Who cares about our fights, our disagreements? None of that matters, just come back, Eitan! Do you hear me? Do you hear me?

2. The first night after the massacre

A hospital room. A NURSE *enters.*

NURSE. Sorry. Visiting hours are over. You have to leave now. Until seven tomorrow morning.

WAHIDA. I'm sorry, I don't speak Hebrew.

NURSE. It's eight o'clock. You have to leave now. Until seven tomorrow morning.

WAHIDA. Will you call me if he wakes up in the night?

NURSE. Do we know where to reach you?

WAHIDA. I lost my phone. You can reach me on Eitan's phone or at the Paradise Hotel. Lions' Gate.

NURSE. You should move closer to the hospital. The army might close off the Muslim Quarter.

WAHIDA. Can I stay here?

NURSE. It's not allowed.

WAHIDA. Just tonight.

NURSE. I'm sorry. The entire floor is occupied by victims of the attack. Many of them will die tonight. The first night after an attack separates the living from the dead. You couldn't handle it. No one can. So we limit the number of people present. Otherwise, we'd fall apart, too. The days ahead are going to be difficult. You have to get some rest. You have to sleep.

WAHIDA. I can't sleep. I replay the scene in my head as soon as I'm alone. I close my eyes and it all comes back, the bridge, the people, the heat, the sun, customs, the body search, an endless loop of images until the explosion.

NURSE. Were you together?

WAHIDA. They had separated us. That's what saved me and probably saved him too. If they hadn't decided to search me, both of us probably would have died on that bus to Jordan. But when the truck attacked, I was still being interrogated. Eitan had told me, I'll wait for you, and we were separated. I didn't see it happen. I was with a woman soldier who was body-searching me when the explosion took place. A horrendous vomiting followed by the smell of burnt flesh. I had never seen so many dead bodies.

NURSE. Are you alone in Israel?

WAHIDA. Yes.

NURSE. Where does his family live?

WAHIDA. Berlin.

NURSE. Have they been notified?

WAHIDA. I'm not the right person to contact them.

NURSE. They have to be notified. Where are you from?

WAHIDA. New York.

NURSE. Contact his parents. That's the first thing to do. You can't face this alone. What's your name?

WAHIDA. Wahida.

EITAN. Wahida?

NURSE. My name is Sigal. Here.

She hands WAHIDA a tablet.

This will help you sleep. If Eitan wakes up, I'll call you. I promise.

The NURSE exits.

3. 46 chromosomes

WAHIDA and EITAN, in the snowbound streets of New York.

EITAN. What does "Wahida" mean?

WAHIDA. The unique. What about "Eitan"?

EITAN. The robust.

WAHIDA. You sure it doesn't mean "the player"?

EITAN. You sure "Wahida" doesn't mean "a genetic monstrosity"?

WAHIDA. That's nice.

EITAN. It's true. You're totally improbable. How is it possible for there to be so many different kinds of living beings? Why are you so beautiful while I'm such a mess?

WAHIDA. That's right, why?

EITAN. Why? Why does an embryo develop to become this or that? I wanted to devote my life to solving that enigma, but what's the point of understanding the origins of the species when your face makes me want to set this street on fire. It's tragic . . .

WAHIDA. It's terrible. Here we are. "This is the end."

Music. They dance.

EITAN. What did you say "Wahida" means? Because if I fall in love with you, how could I bear the idea of losing you?

WAHIDA. But you're not going to fall in love.

EITAN. That's easy for you to say. You're looking at me. But for me, looking at you, what choice do I have?

WAHIDA. Is this a declaration?

EITAN. It's a realization. No matter how hard I keep telling myself, like Ava Hoss, who's directing my research on the evolution of the microsatellite codes in primates, always says: genetically speaking, there is only a forty percent difference between you and the yeast used to bake donuts, but I can't take my eyes off your face.

WAHIDA. Did you just compare me to yeast?

EITAN. I could compare you to a frog and it wouldn't change a thing.

WAHIDA. I love the way you talk to girls. What about the soul?

EITAN. A matter of genomes. There's no hierarchy in the cellular world.

WAHIDA. You make identity seem simple.

EITAN. Forty-six chromosomes.

WAHIDA. And love?

EITAN. Love, the Holocaust, testimony, memory, friendship . . . Forty-six chromosomes.

WAHIDA. Promises, tenderness, humour?

EITAN. Forty-six chromosomes.

WAHIDA. Youth?

EITAN. Forty-six chromosomes.

WAHIDA. My face? My skin.

EITAN. Forty-six chromosomes.

WAHIDA. My lips?

EITAN. Forty-six chromosomes.

They kiss. Make love.

4. Perfect skin

WAHIDA enters a café. A cartoon is playing on television in Hebrew.

WAHIDA. A coffee, please.

WAITER. It's midnight, I'll be closing soon.

The WAITER exits. Beat. EDEN, a young Israeli woman soldier enters and sits down facing WAHIDA.

EDEN. How long have you been in Israel?

WAHIDA. One week.

EDEN. Where were you staying?

WAHIDA. The Paradise Hotel.

EDEN. Alone?

WAHIDA. With my boyfriend.

EDEN. His name?

WAHIDA. Eitan Zimmerman.

EDEN. Is he Israeli?

WAHIDA. No, German.

EDEN. Where is he?

WAHIDA. He went through customs and he's waiting for me beside the bus.

Beat. EDEN *is taking notes.*

EDEN. Where are you going?

WAHIDA. Jordan.

EDEN. Why?

WAHIDA. As tourists.

EDEN. Married?

WAHIDA. No.

EDEN. What were the two of you doing in Israel?

WAHIDA. My boyfriend came to meet his grandmother.

EDEN. Her name?

WAHIDA. Leah Kimhi.

EDEN. Did you see her?

WAHIDA. He needed to see her alone.

EDEN. Why?

WAHIDA. They were meeting for the first time. It was touchy.

EDEN. Did you see anyone else during your stay?

WAHIDA. Gershon Avnery.

EDEN. Who's that?

WAHIDA. A specialist in ancient Arabic literature in the Islamic and Middle East department at the National Library of Israel.

EDEN. What did you talk about?

WAHIDA. A sixteenth-century manuscript.

EDEN. Why?

WAHIDA. That book is at the heart of my thesis.

EDEN. So you weren't here to accompany your boyfriend?

WAHIDA. I took advantage of the trip.

EDEN. What's the subject of your thesis?

WAHIDA. Complicated.

EDEN. We've got time.

WAHIDA. A sixteenth-century Moroccan diplomat kidnapped and given to Pope Leo X who converted him to Christianity. I defend the hypothesis that his conversion was a dissimulation.

EDEN. Where are you studying?

WAHIDA. Columbia University. New York.

EDEN flips through WAHIDA's *passport.*

EDEN. Does Eitan have a job?

WAHIDA. A researcher.

EDEN. In what field?

WAHIDA. Genetics.

EDEN. Are you spying on him?

WAHIDA. What?!

EDEN. Who are you working for?

WAHIDA. I don't understand . . .

EDEN. How long have you had a US passport?

WAHIDA. I'm an American citizen!

EDEN. What were you doing in Egypt, Tunisia, Algeria and Morocco?

WAHIDA. Research for my thesis.

EDEN. Do you fuck a Jew for your thesis too? An Arab? Are you an Arab?

WAHIDA. No . . . Yes . . .

EDEN. No? Yes? Is that Eitan's picture on your phone?

WAHIDA. Yes.

EDEN. What's a girl like you doing with a guy like that? Is he rich? Famous? Are you spying on him?

WAHIDA. Of course not!

EDEN. Who are you working for? Who is that man?

WAHIDA. I told you, he's my boyfriend.

EDEN. The diplomat! Your thesis! Who is the man?

WAHIDA. Al-Hasan ibn Muhammad al-Wazzan.

EDEN. Is he your boss? Is he involved in terrorist activities?

WAHIDA. He died five hundred years ago!

EDEN. I don't know. Maybe. Tell me about him.

WAHIDA. What do you want me to say?

EDEN. Tell me what you know. Where was he born?

WAHIDA. In Granada. In Spain.

EDEN. When?

WAHIDA. Around 1486. But he grew up in Fez in Morocco.

EDEN. What did he do?

WAHIDA. He was a diplomat. I already told you that.

EDEN. You're writing a thesis about some guy who died five hundred years ago and who was just a diplomat? What was his doctrine, his ideology?

WAHIDA. There was no doctrine, no ideology . . . Listen, my boyfriend is waiting for me . . . Okay . . . In 1518, on his way back from a pilgrimage to Mecca, he was captured by a Christian pirate . . . The pirate, instead of selling this high-level diplomat as an ordinary slave, decides to offer him to Pope Leo X as a present. The pope, impressed by his brilliant mind, offers to grant the prisoner freedom in exchange for his conversion. So with a little splash of water on his forehead, Hasan al-Wazzan changes religion and becomes Leo Africanus. His whole life is like that. Neither destiny nor chance, somewhere in between. A bridge. He travels and meets the humblest and the most powerful people, he encounters various tribes, learns languages. A contemporary of da Vinci and Machiavelli, he lives for ten years in Rome where he completes an immense geographical treatise introducing Europeans to an Africa hitherto unknown, and he counts both Jews and Christians among his friends. When he finally returns home, we lose sight of him . . . No one knows where he died. His tomb has never been found. He disappeared, evaporated.

EDEN. And why are you interested in him?

WAHIDA. I believe his story offers answers to questions that are relevant today.

EDEN. What questions?

WAHIDA. Is it really important to cling to our lost identities? What is a life lived between two worlds? What is a migrant? A refugee? A mutant?

Beat.

EDEN. Take off your clothes.

WAHIDA hesitates. She stands. Takes off her jacket. EDEN dons a pair of latex gloves.

Take off your dress.

EDEN helps her with the straps. WAHIDA removes her dress.

Take everything off.

WAHIDA takes off her underwear. EDEN sets WAHIDA's clothes and belongings aside. She stares at WAHIDA.

Eitan must lose his mind.

EDEN exits. Beat. EDEN returns.

Open your mouth.

She examines WAHIDA's mouth.

Spread your legs. I'm going to touch you. Wider.

WAHIDA is on the verge of tears.

I'm going to touch you.

EDEN removes her gloves and places her hands on WAHIDA's back. She kisses WAHIDA's back. WAHIDA turns around suddenly. EDEN kisses WAHIDA. Explosion.

Back in the coffee shop, the TELEVISION is broadcasting the news in Hebrew.

TELEVISION. No group has claimed responsibility for the attack and although everything suggests it is the work of Palestinian terrorists, the ramming vehicle comes from the Israeli settlement of Beit Jarod, recently declared illegal by the supreme court, which has ordered its evacuation. The international community has condemned the terrorist attack on the Allenby Bridge and is urging Israeli and

Palestinian authorities to exercise extreme caution. The US secretary of state and the Russian minister of foreign affairs have warned the Palestinian National Authority against any action that could ignite tensions in the region. Until the results of the genetic testing being done on the remains of the kamikaze driver are released, the prime minister's office is preparing to cordon off East Jerusalem and forbid all traffic to and from Palestinian territories.

WAHIDA. How much do I owe you?

WAITER. Thirteen shekels.

TELEVISION. The attack, which took place this morning at 10:53 at the border checkpoint on the Allenby Bridge between Israel and Jordan, claimed seventy-eight lives and left some one hundred wounded, twenty in critical condition. Six Israeli soldiers were killed.

WAHIDA. What are they saying?

WAITER. They're talking about the Allenby Bridge attack. They're doing genetic testing and cordoning off certain quarters.

WAHIDA. Have they closed off the Muslim Quarter?

WAITER. Not yet but it won't be long. The army has arrived. You shouldn't go there.

WAHIDA. Thank you.

WAITER. Good night.

WAHIDA exits. The WAITER turns off the TV.

5. A phone call

In the street, WAHIDA *takes out* EITAN's *mobile phone and dials.*

WAHIDA. Hello. Is that Mrs. Leah Kimhi? / My name is Wahida, I'm your grandson Eitan's friend. / Yes, you do, I came to see you earlier and you slammed the door in my face . . . Hello? . . . Shit, what a bitch!

She dials again.

Mrs. Kimhi . . . This is Wahida. I hope you listen to my message. I'm on my way to your house and if you don't let me in, I'm going to break your door down.

WAHIDA *hangs up.*

6. A door

WAHIDA *is banging on* LEAH's *door.*

WAHIDA. Open the door! Open the door! I know you're there. Open the door, goddammit! Open this door, you bitch!

LEAH. Stop! You're going to hurt yourself and you'll damage my door.

WAHIDA. Open the door.

LEAH. What do you want?

WAHIDA. Eitan is dying.

LEAH. Call his family.

WAHIDA. You are his family.

> *WAHIDA knocks again. LEAH opens the door.*

LEAH. What do you want from me?

WAHIDA. You have to contact his parents.

LEAH. I don't know who you're talking about.

WAHIDA. Eitan's parents.

LEAH. Who is Eitan?

WAHIDA. Are you fucking crazy or what? He spent the week with you.

LEAH. A young man showed up. I didn't know who he was. I didn't even know he existed.

WAHIDA. You talked to him. You ate together.

LEAH. When?

WAHIDA. Every day.

LEAH. He told you that?

WAHIDA. Yes.

LEAH. He lied.

WAHIDA. Why would he do that?

LEAH. I don't know. But I never saw him again and he lied to you.

WAHIDA. He lied to me?

LEAH. He lied to you.

WAHIDA. I don't understand. You never spoke to each other?

LEAH. No. Now go away.

WAHIDA. That's what he came for. He thought you could answer his questions.

LEAH. He was wrong.

WAHIDA. He wanted you to talk to him about his father.

LEAH. Go away!

WAHIDA. Who is David, your son?

LEAH. I don't know. Just leave!

WAHIDA. Yes, you do know, and Eitan knows that you know.

LEAH. That I know what?

WAHIDA. Who his father is. Who David is—who your son is! They left Berlin and came to visit Eitan in New York for Passover. Your ex-husband . . . I've forgotten his name . . .

LEAH. So have I!

WAHIDA. Etgar! And David and Norah, Eitan's parents. Didn't he tell you? Didn't he tell you what happened?

LEAH. No. What happened?

WAHIDA. The meal. Passover. The Seder. He didn't tell you anything? This year Eitan insisted it was their turn to travel. "I'm always the one who goes back to Berlin to see you, this time you come to see me. I'll show you around the campus, the laboratories, the library. I'll introduce you to my friends." So they came and everyone started talking about longitudes and latitudes: Berlin is farther north than New York and it's already spring there while New York is as far south as Marseille and there's a foot of snow. Eitan took them to visit museums, parks, synagogues and the Statue of Liberty. He made every effort. He even invited a rabbi to the Seder, to make them happy, to respect the tradition.

LEAH. Why?

WAHIDA. To introduce them to me. Me! To tell them: I've been in love with a woman for two years and that woman's name is Wahida.

7. Seder

New York. Passover Seder.

ETGAR. DAVID. NORAH, *a* RABBI, EITAN.

In their midst, WAHIDA *takes* LEAH *through the story.*

NORAH. Wahida? Eitan has always known how to surprise us.

ETGAR. Eitan, my boy, let me kiss you. You are God's gift to me in my old age, my joy, my treasure, my darling.

RABBI. Your son has great respect for you.

NORAH. So you were aware of this?

RABBI. Eitan came to ask my advice.

NORAH. Ah ha! And you suggested that he organize this meal.

RABBI. A fine occasion to share his news.

ETGAR. And what fine news!

NORAH. You're incredible, Eitan.

ETGAR. What wonderful news!

NORAH. Where did you find this rabbi? You speak German so well!

RABBI. My German is just adequate. My family is originally from South Africa and they immigrated to Rumania, but German-speaking Rumania was annexed to Hungary. My grandfather was an important rabbi. I didn't know him, of course, he went up in smoke with everyone else, but my mother worshiped him. In a way, I became a rabbi to make my mother happy. She wasn't able to take care of me because of her mental illness. I was still a child when she stopped speaking English and only expressed herself in German, so I had to learn the language to speak to her.

NORAH. A touching story.

RABBI. Thank you. So, shall we resume . . . "When Pharaoh, king of Egypt, refused to let us go, with a mighty hand and an outstretched arm, the Lord our God brought us out of Egypt. Had the Lord not taken our ancestors out of Egypt, we and our children and our grandchildren would still be slaves in Egypt."

DAVID. You couldn't have hurt us more if you had tried.

ETGAR. David, don't go against life.

DAVID. Who's going against life?

ETGAR. Your son is happy, that's what matters.

DAVID. There are things we're not ready for. I'm not saying they're bad, just that we're not ready.

EITAN. I'm not asking for your blessing.

DAVID. That's not the point. It's your life, you are free, no law today forbids you from loving whomever you want, but there is another law, a more ancient law, that originates in the blood of our ancestors and makes us responsible for each other.

EITAN. I don't want to feel guilty!

DAVID. That's where you're wrong.

EITAN. I'm wrong?

DAVID. Yes, you're wrong. You're mistaken.

EITAN. I'm talking about love and you're talking to me about guilt.

NORAH. Your father's talking about the guilt that is a manifestation of a phylogenetic function related to decreed rules. He's talking about guilt as a formative emotion that makes us more empathetic, more sensitive to the suffering of others. Was I wrong to break the rules, and how can I make up for my mistake?

EITAN. C'mon, Mama, I'm your son, not your patient.

NORAH. That doesn't change a thing. Your father is right. The absence of guilt is characteristic of the psychopath for whom the other is a mere object. I see countless cases every day in my practice.

DAVID. I'm talking about guilt as a gift. The particular guilt of our people that no other people can feel because it is born of the suffering of our fathers and grandfathers. The guilt of the survivor.

It guides all our choices and frees me from everything. I think of those who came before me and I realize that I don't know what suffering means. They are giants and we are dwarves and if we see the world it's because they are carrying us on their shoulders. And if I ever have to go through what they did, I'll remind myself that I am simply following in their footsteps.

RABBI. We had reached the escape from Egypt. We should return to that.

ETGAR. Good idea.

DAVID. How can this woman hope to make you happy?

EITAN. How can you say that? Because she isn't—

DAVID. What?

EITAN. What?

DAVID. Why are you asking me?

EITAN. Say it!

DAVID. It's obvious.

NORAH. He's asking you a question. Answer.

DAVID. It's too painful for me to hear what he's telling me.

EITAN. She's an Arab? Is that it?

DAVID. Don't make me say what I don't want to say! I didn't insult her—I don't want to insult her—I'm sure she's a fine person, undoubtedly marvellous since you love her!

EITAN. She's not Jewish?

DAVID. Don't make me say—

EITAN. It's ridiculous! Such a cliché! I don't believe it!

DAVID. No, she isn't Jewish!

EITAN. So you've said it!

DAVID. Yes, I've said it, stop contradicting me, yes, that's it, she's not Jewish. She's not part of our circle, our garden. Shit! Shit! There! You're making me exclude when I don't want to exclude anyone. Do you think I like saying that a human being is or isn't? Saying that to my son?

ETGAR. David, it's time for the prayer.

DAVID. The prayer means telling your son the truth!

RABBI. The truth is that there isn't only one truth.

ETGAR. You're right, but you can't impose your truth.

DAVID. But I can impose upon him the truth that you transmitted to me. Eitan, look at his eyes, his hands.

ETGAR. That's enough.

DAVID. This man watched his mother be murdered by a bullet shot with total indifference into the crowd disembarking from a livestock car, and ever since that shot rang out, whether you like it or not, survival is our responsibility, our duty—mine, yours, your children's and your children's children's duty, since no one else will carry the taste of the ashes of our families who disappeared.

EITAN. How does one thing exclude the other?

DAVID. You cannot participate in this disappearance.

EITAN. How does loving mean participating?

DAVID. Transmission, flesh and blood.

EITAN. What do you know about flesh and blood?

DAVID. How do you become a Jew, Eitan? Through whom? Through whom are you a Jew?

EITAN. Through my mother.

NORAH. This is leading nowhere. The two of you are poisoning my life.

DAVID. And the children you'll have together, how can they be born Jewish with a mother with a name like hers?

EITAN. So what if my children aren't Jewish! I don't give a damn.

DAVID. That's what I'm saying.

EITAN. So much the better, who gives a shit! They'll be free.

DAVID. You see! You're participating in the disappearance and you're not ashamed. You're insulting us and you're insulting your grandfather's memory.

ETGAR. No, he isn't!

DAVID. And you dare tell me that in the language of our murderers.

NORAH. It's his mother's language and it has nothing to do with murderers. Stop provoking him. Stop! It makes me sick seeing the two of you like that. Let him love her, for God's sake. Who says it's going to last? It's not going to last. He's not telling us that she's pregnant—she's not pregnant, is she? Is she pregnant?

EITAN. Mama!

NORAH. She's not pregnant! He'll get over it. It's a good experience for him, it'll expose him to other cultures.

EITAN. No, I won't get over it.

NORAH. Be quiet!

EITAN. I wouldn't have asked you to come if it was just a passing experience!

DAVID. So why did you bring us here?

EITAN. Would you have preferred that I announce it by email?

NORAH. Why are you doing this?

EITAN. Doing what?

NORAH. You know us. You know our lives. Just think about it. Shit!

EITAN. What do you want me to think about? I love her. It's simple.

NORAH. I love her. It's simple. Are you stupid or what?! This will destroy us. Can't you see that? It's not philosophical, historical, political, theological or psychoanalytical. It's simple all right! It sets us against each other, separates us, and it's killing me.

EITAN. How can loving separate people? How can my telling you kill you?

NORAH. It's not what you're telling me that kills me, it's your way of forcing us to kill each other that's killing me. I can't tell you to stop loving that girl against your father's wishes, since I loved your father against my father's wishes. Do you hear me? You're doing to your father what I did to mine. You leave me no choice. I'm forced to agree with you and forced to be against your father and I hate that. Not because I don't love you, on the contrary, but I also love your father and I feel torn! Eitan! Fucking hell! We love you. I wanted your life to be an attack on my parents' ideology: their principles, their shitty communism, their shitty East in the shadow of the shitty wall with their shitty committees, their shitty speeches and their shitty dogmas that gutted my youth. I was devoured, swallowed up and digested and dumped into the shitholes of my parents' ideals, their utopias and dreams. So when I introduced your father to them, it was like I was spitting in their face.

EITAN. So? Exactly!

NORAH. Yes. Exactly! Don't you see how you've trapped me? You are spitting in your father's face and I can't choose between you.

ETGAR. Norah, you can't both be against him.

EITAN. I'm not spitting in my father's face.

NORAH. Yes, you are. You're spitting in his face twice! She's not Jewish, and she's an Arab. I don't give a damn and I've got nothing against Arabs, but she's an Arab, so she's his enemy and you can't blame your father for thinking that! Could you blame a Jew for being devastated in 1946 if his son announced that he was going to marry a German girl, a fair, blond, blue-eyed German girl! It's engraved in our reptilian brains! No tribe can stand seeing one of their children leave for the enemy camp. Group identity! It's the malady, the curse of all humans. My parents hid the fact that we were Jewish from us, not to protect us but because they wanted us to be communists! Communists! Our identity was communism! Group identity! Diktat! I hate that bludgeoning! It's the incinerator! The obliterator. The steamroller! Have you ever seen a steamroller spread asphalt on a pretty country road? Nothing can stop it. And we are the little ants on the pretty country road. What can an ant do to stop a steamroller? Nothing. That's how it is. You have to surrender. Today Arabs are your father's enemies. That's it. It's unfortunate, but it simply is. There is an ocean of Arabs bent on the destruction of Israel. That's no detail. It simply is. So you, for whom everything is a matter of molecules, you can't tell your father, the father you love, who you're in love with, without understanding that it will devastate him!

EITAN. Well, I'm in love. It simply is.

DAVID. So, come spit in my face!

EITAN. Aren't you insulting me? Spitting in my face?

DAVID. If you want to speak to me, speak to me in Hebrew.

EITAN. I'll speak to you in whatever language I please. You're crushing me, you're both crushing me, and I don't understand why.

RABBI. We are all crushed, Eitan.

EITAN. Then why doesn't my grandfather, who is here, who escaped the ashes of the camps, why doesn't he crush me? And why is it the words of my father, who did not know or live through those events, why is it his words that smother me? And why is it my mother's love that kills me, when she's capable of telling me, I understand you, but I won't defend you. Why?

ETGAR. Your parents are crazy about you, Eitan.

EITAN. Then why don't they welcome me? You talk to me about transmission when that's what my life is about! Why are you smiling? What's so funny?! Do you realize who you're saying that word to? You say it but you don't know the true meaning of that word. You poison my life, telling me that I should take responsibility for past suffering, while I am in the best position to know there is no transmission of suffering. None whatsoever. Suffering cannot be transmitted from one generation to another! Everything is accidental, do you hear me! Let me say it in Hebrew! *The experiences of a human being during his lifetime do not affect his chromosomes, no matter how brutal those experiences are!* No worry can be the cause of any cancer, nothing is registered, nothing is transformed. Our genes are indifferent to our experiences. Totally indifferent! Your chromosomes do not carry your father's trauma. All of Auschwitz did not affect a single gene, not a speck of my grandfather's DNA. Listen to me: in 1966, when your father impregnated your mother, there was no concentration camp in his sperm. Don't leave, sit down and listen to me! Forget your notion of transmission! The only transmission that exists is genetic and genetics are deaf and blind to any emotion or pain. That doesn't exist in flesh and blood, only in the head! That's all cheap psychology. An education that cultivates guilt because we haven't found a better way to teach children about the past, without boring them or traumatizing them, and if we traumatize them, it's because we want them to be traumatized. We don't want them to escape. So we invented the word "transmission." "Transmission" sounds better than "assassination," so we talk to them about "memory, our ancestors' legacy, the weight of the past," and we're killing them. Because of our pain, our deep, dark sorrow. How else do you explain that we never learn the lesson, generation after generation? If traumas affected the genes we transmit to our children, do you really think our people would subject another people to the oppression we were subjected to before? I can't believe the two of you aren't thrilled. How often did you worry about my lack of feeling, my lack of poetry and imagination? No one, absolutely no one except maybe my grandfather, believed that some day an idiot like me could feel what I feel for another human being. If I lose her, I'll die. Do you hear me? I respect my grandfather's suffering, and yours, and that of my people. I understand the birth of Israel and its importance and saying that brings tears to my eyes, but nothing can match love. Is what I just said so outrageous? Forget it. Forget what I said.

ETGAR. David, what I lived through is mine.

DAVID. Not just yours.

ETGAR. We don't really know each other . . . that's what I meant.

DAVID. I don't know. It's Passover. Our most beautiful holiday, even if it's the one that always made me unhappy as a child. I never found the *afikomen*. And today, trying to explain the inexplicable to my son, I feel like the child who can't find the *afikomen* again. But one thing is clear. After everything we've gone through, we cannot allow ourselves to be subjected to the laws of chance . . .

LEAH. What chance was he talking about?

WAHIDA. I don't know . . . I was standing outside on the landing for an hour, not daring to ring the bell, unable to leave, unable to stay. I could hear them arguing through love and pain, incapable of understanding each other, drifting farther and farther apart. I sent a text to Eitan: "Outside on the landing." And I waited. A young woman, empty-handed. Or almost. Holding a thesis on an obscure sixteenth-century diplomat with an unpronounceable name, Hasan ibn Muhammad al-Wazzan, who was kidnapped and made a life of dissimulation, and there I was on that landing, wondering whether people my age aren't all like that, caught between two storeys, listening to dreams collapse.

LEAH. You shouldn't have waited. You should have rung the bell, gone inside, kidnapped the man you love and left without looking back . . .

DAVID. Do you see this knife?

EITAN. I see it.

DAVID. If I stab you in the throat, what will happen?

EITAN. You'll be guilty of infanticide.

DAVID. Make a life with this woman and you'll be guilty of parricide . . .

> *DAVID exits, followed by NORAH, the RABBI and ETGAR. EITAN stands up and begins to clear the table, placing the cutlery used by his relatives in separate plastic bags.*

LEAH. What is he doing?

WAHIDA. He's keeping the spoons. Placing each one in a separate plastic bag. For a fraction of a second, he must have known, he must have sensed it, a burning flash of insight, I don't know. His scientific turn of mind makes it hard to be sure.

EITAN. I can't believe that man is my father!

WAHIDA. Undoubtedly a way of taking revenge, reducing his parents to mere miasma fit for nothing but a scientific experiment.

LEAH. What experiment?

WAHIDA. Reducing his parents to samples. Sequencing them. Labelling them in test tubes. To compare their DNA.

LEAH. An eye for an eye, a tooth for a tooth.

WAHIDA. The experiment confirmed, to his great disappointment, that he was the son of his father and mother, but it also revealed that that was not true of his own father. David was not Etgar's son. The whole family went back to Berlin. Eitan tried to remember if anyone had ever insinuated anything, a detail. Nothing. Was everyone aware of the truth, or not? Did David know, or not? Did Etgar know, or not? Asking that question, revealing the results of his experiment without knowing if they knew seemed too dangerous. That's when he thought of you. The only one who knows is the woman who carried David in her womb.

LEAH. That's why he came?

WAHIDA. And that's why he's dying! So you have to take responsibility and call your son in Berlin and tell him to get on the first plane with his wife, and if he asks you why, you have to find the words to tell him that his son is lying between life and death.

WAHIDA exits. LEAH remains alone.

8. The unreal bougainvillea

*Armed from head to toe, EDEN is standing outside the door
to WAHIDA's hotel room. WAHIDA appears.*

EDEN. Sorry. Do you recognize me?

WAHIDA. Yes.

EDEN. We were together when the bomb exploded.

WAHIDA. Yes.

EDEN. Sorry about what happened.

WAHIDA. Why did you come?

EDEN. I wanted to return your passport and your phone. After
the explosion, when you left, I thought I was delirious. At dawn
the army will begin to invade the Palestinian territories. When
they issued the order, I vomited. But when I vomit, everything
comes out except that horror. I really wanted to apologize for what
happened. It was against everything I was taught. I didn't see it
coming. Everything exploded, before the explosion, the minute I
put my hand on your skin, and suddenly it was as if nothing made
sense anymore, nothing mattered except that softness. I wanted
to go on caressing and hold that moment inside me. Do you
understand? When you discover something like that, it's impossible to let it disappear from your life forever. I have to leave . . .
Eitan? . . . Did he die?

WAHIDA. No.

EDEN. Oh! Thank you. I spent the whole day counting bodies, helping the wounded. There was a bougainvillea in bloom, brilliant scarlet, in the middle of the shouts, the screams. I thought about this beauty in the sunlight, but it was nothing. No beauty, no bougainvillea, just the bloody remains of a human body caught in the barbed wire.

WAHIDA. What's your name?

EDEN. Eden. My name is Eden.

WAHIDA. You can stay with me, if you want.

EDEN. Yes!

WAHIDA. Eden in the Paradise Hotel.

EDEN. They've issued the order but what is left of this night is ours. At least these few hours are ours.

WAHIDA. Talk to me.

EDEN. I've forgotten how to talk.

WAHIDA. And I can't stay silent anymore.

Bombs. Fighter planes.

II
BIRD OF CHANCE

9. The anonymity of joy and sorrow

EITAN's hospital room. Outside the window, a milky-white sky. Typical sounds of hospital apparatuses. Bouquet of red flowers in a yellow vase. A NURSE'S AIDE is bathing EITAN. WAHIDA is at his bedside.

WAHIDA. Leah called your parents. I don't know what they said to each other, I just know that the first plane from Berlin has landed. A trap is snapping shut. I'm wavering, Eitan. I'm trying to fall back on my thesis but it all seems so false, so contrived. I went through my notes again and in the middle of my mess, I came across a photo of Raphael's fresco depicting an elephant. I had forgotten that detail. Four years before al-Wazzan was offered as a present to the pope, the king of Portugal presented the same pope with a white elephant from India. Hanno. That was his name. He was present at all the festivals, all the processions, and images of him can still be found on Roman fountains, and on the fresco Raphael painted in his honour. Wazzan: nothing. Barely a trace. And nothing about those who were kidnapped with him. Five centuries later, this hospital ward is full of disasters, every room is full of people stricken with anxiety. We will never know their names. I think of your parents, of the call they received in the middle of the night announcing that their son is hovering between life and death. I think of their love for you, and I feel crushed, crushed by the enormous anonymity of human suffering, while the records of that goddamn elephant could fill this room.

Al-WAZZAN *is present.*

WAZZAN. Why does that poor elephant make you so angry?

WAHIDA. Why am I interested in you, Hasan ibn Muhammad al-Wazzan? Whose life can my work change? Who could be consoled by it? Why should I give a damn whether you faked your conversion or not?

WAZZAN. You're right.

WAHIDA. My friends keep asking me when I'm going to finish my novel. They think you're a fictional character.

WAZZAN. Yes, Wahida . . . The past contains secret clues. You think my life will teach you something, but my life, like yours, is strewn with missing links. You are right: a name on a stone tells us nothing about that person's joys and sorrows, and cemeteries are full of anonymous lives. In the middle of these ruins, one elephant was rescued by History because he was the object of adulation, a source of joy for human beings, an enchantment in difficult lives . . . we should be happy for that elephant.

LEAH enters. The NURSE'S AIDE exits.

LEAH. His parents have arrived. And they're not going to be a pretty sight.

WAHIDA. I'm leaving.

LEAH. You're staying. Enough is enough. I haven't seen my son in thirty-five years. Do you think I feel like staying?

WAHIDA. What are you going to tell them? That I'm your granddaughter?

LEAH. The truth.

WAHIDA. That will only make things worse.

LEAH. Everything has a price in life. You think loving a Jew is like loving a cupcake?

WAHIDA. I don't love "a Jew," I love Eitan!

LEAH. When you love someone, you don't run away.

WAHIDA. They'll want to be alone with their son.

LEAH. What are you afraid of?

WAHIDA. This is all my fault!

LEAH. Did you ever take a look at yourself?

WAHIDA. No.

LEAH. You should. Your face alone is an atomic bomb. You have a weapon of mass destruction and instead of using it to defend your love, you stand there asking for permission, acting so sweet, the perfect bride with your slutty little ass in your slutty tight jeans, as if you don't know what you trigger.

WAHIDA. Soon I'll be old and ugly like you.

LEAH. You should get drunk and get laid by a real man. Suck a big dick. That would loosen you up.

WAHIDA. I've rarely met anyone as mean as you.

LEAH. You shouldn't have come knocking on my door.

WAHIDA. Let me know if he wakes up.

LEAH. How can he without you? You came to see me. You told me to take responsibility. Now it's your turn. Face it and play your part. You, the young woman, me the old bitch. Not the other way around.

WAHIDA. Everything's ruined, don't you see that?

LEAH. You have no idea who you're talking to.

    WAHIDA *exits.*

10. Introduction and reunion

LEAH is alone at EITAN's bedside. Beat. She caresses his hand. DAVID and NORAH enter with their suitcases, over-dressed for the climate. LEAH turns her back on them. DAVID rushes over to EITAN's bed while NORAH freezes, unable to move.

DAVID. Where's the doctor?

LEAH. He should be here any minute now.

DAVID. Norah, this is Leah. My mother.

LEAH. So you're David's wife?

NORAH. I'm sorry, my Hebrew is awful.

LEAH. Don't worry, it's mutual. I hate everything German: cars, language, gas, trains and soap. How was your trip? I'm sorry about your son. All this is very new for me, Norah. I have no sense of family and absolutely no maternal instinct. David was a teenager the last time we saw each other. He came to visit me the summer after the divorce. Did he tell you?

NORAH. No.

LEAH. He hasn't changed much. A bit of a belly. He looks like an old man. I wouldn't have recognized him.

NORAH. Did you know Eitan?

LEAH. They called and told me that my son's son was in the hospital.

DAVID. Have you spoken to the doctors?

LEAH. No one's available.

DAVID. It's clear you don't know what it's like to have a child.

LEAH. Take a look inside the other rooms and you'll understand. This is a psychiatric country, Norah, it's the same after every attack. We forget who we are and we mistake everyone for someone else.

DAVID. What are we doing here? Why are we here?

LEAH. Back when David came to see me, Palestinians were exploding in the middle of crowds, in buses and sidewalk cafés. So we built the wall and we were safe until the stabbings began. That was before the nightmare of the entwined teenage couples. You heard about that, right? An Israeli girl from Tel Aviv and a Palestinian boy from Bethlehem, both of them sixteen years old, blew themselves up hugging each other, because their families disapproved of their love. It was so horrendously beautiful, so terribly moving, other couples their age began to imitate them. It went on for months. People started to panic at the slightest kiss. Our government tried to prove there were no Jews involved, that they were all Arabs, but that wasn't the case. When the blood revealed an unspeakable mix in their genealogy, their DNA, or whatever, they stopped testing because they were proving that all of us, Jews and Arabs, were all the same. So they invented the new brand of Palestinian terrorist who used some kind of drug made in Iran, a love potion that inhibits all willpower and leads to the death of young Israelis disguised as Romeo and Juliet kamikazes. When it was simply a case of love. Or lack of love. That's why the attack on the Allenby Bridge where your son almost died hasn't shocked anybody. On the contrary. It's reassuring, back to business as usual. At last, a "vintage" attack where the Jews can accuse the Arabs and the Arabs accuse the settlers.

DAVID. I don't know what is more unbearable: seeing Eitan in that bed or seeing you in this room.

NORAH. Mrs. Zimmerman . . .

LEAH. Not that name!

NORAH. Why did Eitan come to Israel?

LEAH. Why not Israel?

NORAH. No one leaves on vacation saying, "Why not Israel?" His passport shows that he arrived here ten days ago.

LEAH. And spring is yet to come.

NORAH. What was he doing on the Allenby Bridge to Jordan?

LEAH. I have no idea. They called me, I came.

DAVID. Fine. Thank you. We're here now. You can leave.

LEAH. That's very nice of you, but I don't need your permission to stay or to go. You see, Norah, I'm a bad mother. You think I'm heartless, you haven't seen a thing. I have contempt for people who care about me. I abandoned my son and that son is your husband, but you, of course, are a wonderful woman.

NORAH. Leah, that's your name, right? I don't think you or I want to know more than we can guess about each other, but let me explain something. David and I spent yesterday evening at the Lars Friedrich gallery in Berlin where we saw the work of a painter who paints using only his sperm. He's one of my patients. He jerks off three times a day and collects his sperm in a little jar. But he paints large canvases. He's Jewish. Like us! And he is haunted by the thought that he might be going against the Torah. The interpretation of Genesis Chapter 38, Verse 9 affirms that a man's sperm must serve life and should not be wasted. So, is a work of art life? Or is artistic creation a waste of a man's sperm? David thinks it is. I don't. We had a huge argument. We went home and went to bed without speaking to each other, until we were awakened by Etgar, who called to tell us that our son who we haven't spoken to since the goddamn Passover meal, our son who we thought was in New York, was actually in Jerusalem and was one of the victims of the attack on the goddamn bridge that separates Israel from Jordan. While we were arguing about a trendy artist's masturbatory ejaculations, our son was fighting for his life. And we didn't know that! Thinking of that time is like thinking of a hole that we'd like to tear out of our skull with a knife and pliers. Do you understand that, Leah? I'm sure you understand.

LEAH. Eitan didn't come here alone. So figure it out.

DAVID. Who was he with?

LEAH. Who do you think?

NORAH. His girlfriend . . . Is she the one who got in touch with you?

LEAH. Yes.

DAVID. And why did she get in touch with you? And why didn't you call me? Why did you call Papa?

LEAH. I didn't want to hear your voice.

DAVID. Still trying to avoid it all?

LEAH. I'm not avoiding anything. I just don't give a damn.

DAVID. You don't give a damn about what happens to Eitan?

LEAH. Who is Eitan? A stranger . . . a stranger . . . and you're a stranger too. And so is this woman who isn't ashamed to talk about another man's sperm in front of her husband. So don't worry. You don't have to feel betrayed.

DAVID. Being abandoned by your mother vaccinates you against betrayal.

LEAH. I'm not your mother. I already told you that.

DAVID. You're so happy when you say that.

LEAH. We don't really know each other. That's what I mean.

DAVID. So who are you? Go ahead, let's hear it, I'm listening!

LEAH. No. You're deaf and you're blind. You don't hear anything. You don't see anything. Just like your father. Where is he, anyhow? Why didn't Etgar come with you?

NORAH. I didn't want him to get up at dawn. He took the following flight.

DOCTOR and MALE NURSES *enter.*

11. Diagnosis

DAVID and NORAH *introduce themselves to the* DOCTOR. *The* MALE NURSES *note the data on the machines: encephalogram, electrocardiogram.*

DOCTOR. Hello. His condition has stabilized, but he suffered a major head injury.

DAVID. Will he wake up?

NORAH. Sorry, but could we speak English?

DOCTOR. Of course. He is out of danger. We were maintaining his coma so we could control his temperature and administer some powerful drugs, but this morning we began the protocol that will allow him to regain consciousness. From now on, it's all up to Eitan. Stay with him. Not all the time. For a while. Speak to him. A bit. In his mother tongue.

DAVID. Hebrew.

NORAH. German. His mother tongue is German.

DOCTOR. What matters is the voices of those dear to him. His parents, his friends.

DAVID. His friends are in Berlin.

NORAH. Or New York.

LEAH. But his fiancée is here.

DOCTOR. The stronger the emotional attachment, the quicker the brain responds. We reconstruct ourselves through affection.

The DOCTOR and the MALE NURSES exit.

DAVID. I don't want to see that girl here!

LEAH. I'll go get her. You'll see, she's lovely.

LEAH exits.

DAVID. This is a nightmare.

Beat. NORAH picks up the remote control and turns on the TELEVISION to the news broadcast in Hebrew.

TELEVISION. Operation Hailstorm has assumed unheard of proportions with the involvement of four thousand soldiers deployed over all the Palestinian territories, reinforced by tanks, fighter jets and marine destroyers. The minister of defence has warned the population: *"We have to be prepared for escalating activity."* And the prime minister announced that *"Israel will do everything in its power to eradicate the Palestinian terrorist organizations once and for all."* Three Israeli soldiers lost their lives last night and five civilians were killed by rockets fired on the town of Nahariyya.

DAVID. Turn that television off!

TELEVISION. . . . Seventy Palestinians have been killed while Arab countries prepare to . . .

NORAH turns off the television.

DAVID. You can't understand it anyway.

NORAH. How did I ever believe I could avoid this?

DAVID. What are you talking about?

NORAH. This country. That vase is so ugly!

DAVID. Where are you going?

NORAH. To deal with the girl . . .

NORAH exits. DAVID opens the window. Fighter jet. He closes the window. He sits down at EITAN's bedside.

12. The first day

Stormy weather outside the window.

DAVID. The world can dissolve, disappear, I don't give a damn . . . The entire universe means less than a single blink of your eyelid. You are all I have. I don't know what I'm saying when I say that, and I don't know why I'm saying that to you, but it's what I feel. I have never felt so alone. It's like a death inside me, a padlock, and your life is the key. Do you remember what I told you? If everything was created during the first six days of Creation, why is the first day different from the others? I told you that in creating the sky and the earth on the first day, God created numbers. You didn't understand. You were right, it was nonsense, seductive and sophisticated like nonsense always is. Now I can see that God made the first day unique so every parent loves his child with a love that precedes everything. By creating this love, God created the pain of seeing the son leave before the father. There should be cupboards where that kind of pain can be locked away. The child cures his parent but when the son disappears, how can one hope to cure the father? The sickness will be eternal. The child is always better than the parent, the son better than the father, you better than me. The proof? The *afikomen*. As a child, I never managed to find the *afikomen*. They could hide it in the most obvious, visible places, right in front of me, and I wouldn't find it. At your very first Seder, you were three years old, you went straight to it without hesitating. Can you hear me, Eitan? I was so surprised. Come back, Eitan, and we'll see. Everything would be possible if you opened your eyes. Everything. Eitan. I beg you. I beg you.

A shower. Rain pelts the windows.

13. Dirty work

NORAH and WAHIDA in the adjacent waiting room.

NORAH. I really didn't want to lay eyes on you, let alone talk to you, but it's always been clear between my husband and me that it's David who suffers most. He's more fragile.

WAHIDA. So you're in charge of the dirty work.

NORAH. Do you love my son?

WAHIDA. I love Eitan.

NORAH. What were the two of you doing on that bridge?

WAHIDA. We were on our way to Amman, before travelling on to Medina and Mecca.

NORAH. Were you hoping to convert him to Islam?

WAHIDA. Do you have so little respect for your son?

NORAH. Please, don't provoke me and don't think you can touch me by appealing to my heart as a mother. I understand why you fell for Eitan. I was as beautiful as you when I was young, and, like you, I didn't know how to manage the beauty that made me want to disfigure myself. For women like us, the solution is to pair up with a simple man, a monosyllabic man in a way, a good husband as they say.

WAHIDA. None of that matters now. Eitan and I will never recover.

NORAH. Recover your love?

WAHIDA. You can reassure your husband.

NORAH. I have nothing against you.

WAHIDA. Neither against nor for. What do you want from me?

NORAH. What was my son, a Jew, going to do in Mecca with an Arab?

WAHIDA. You wouldn't understand.

NORAH. Why?

WAHIDA. You don't believe in love.

NORAH. Love. You make it sound so cute. Like a little girl dressing her doll. Do you think I'm one of your girlfriends? You want to talk about our problems with boys? Share our little secrets? Do you have any idea what's hidden inside the labyrinths of a fifty-year-old woman who sees her son lying between life and death? It breaks your heart, and without a heart there is no love, only the disaster of the life you tried to build, the life you fought for and that is falling apart before your very eyes. And you don't understand why. So if you don't want me to strangle you, don't talk to me about love. What's your name?

WAHIDA. Wahida.

NORAH. Wahida. How pretty. Exotic. Look at me, Wahida. Look at my face. What do you see?

WAHIDA. The face of a sad woman.

NORAH. How sweet of you. No, it's the face of a dog. Not the face of a woman, a human being, a mother, a psychiatrist, a Jew or a German, no. The face of a she-dog. A bitch prepared to bite to save her world. And my world is being destroyed and I don't know what's destroying it. It's hanging by a thread, and for the thread to hold, I need to know what happened. So, Wahida, my exotic beauty from *A Thousand and One Nights*, my dear, my sweetheart, you're going to lead me out of the fog, you're going to tell me what has happened since our visit to New York. Tell me why my son suddenly took leave from his lab and, most of all, first of all, you're going to explain in detail exactly what the two of you came to do here.

WAHIDA. It's not up to me to explain that.

Beat.

Eitan wanted to talk to his grandmother.

NORAH. Why?

Beat.

Why?!

WAHIDA. I wish it were me lying there. Everything would be better.

NORAH. David also believes that things could be *better* in life. He's like his father, Etgar. He says if one person had died instead of another, things would have been better. That if someone had lived longer, things would have been better. He's superstitious. He believes in destiny.

WAHIDA. Except David wasn't fathered by Etgar.

Beat.

You didn't know that? . . . Does David know? Does Etgar know? Leah knows for sure. The female animal knows who her offspring are. A mother knows who she is and who she isn't. That's what Eitan came to ask Leah, but Leah slammed the door in his face. If David had allowed Eitan to introduce the woman he loves that evening in New York, you wouldn't have been reduced to being nothing but a she-dog today. Now the dirty work has to be done.

14. A way of being seen

LEAH enters.

LEAH. If you're discussing where the wedding should be held, you better hurry because they're cordoning off the city. The Muslim Quarter is no longer accessible, more missiles have been fired from south Lebanon and they're worried about new terrorist attacks.

NORAH. What about the airport?

LEAH. Probably chaos.

NORAH. Do you think they'll close it?

LEAH. It will reopen.

DAVID enters.

DAVID. What's going on?

LEAH. We're talking about the wedding, but we can't decide on the menu: kosher or halal?

NORAH. They might close down the airport.

DAVID. Papa must have arrived already.

He takes out his mobile and dials.

Who knows where he is now!

NORAH. He's on his way. David, listen to me.

DAVID. Why did he come? He didn't need to come!

LEAH. I'm the one who insisted that he come.

DAVID. What?!

NORAH. David!

DAVID. Why did you do that?

NORAH. David, we have to get out of here before they close down the airport. There must be a way to have Eitan transferred to Berlin by plane.

DAVID. What are you talking about?

He turns off his mobile.

Voice mail.

NORAH. Maybe his flight is late.

DAVID. Shit!

NORAH. Maybe the battery is dead or he didn't hear it ring. David, we have to try to leave. If they close everything down, we'll be stuck here.

DAVID. *(to WAHIDA)* What was the point of coming here anyway? What the hell came over you? What were you trying to prove to him?

NORAH. Stop!

DAVID. And what the fuck were you doing on that goddamn bridge? Did you get married, was this your honeymoon? First Jerusalem, then Mecca?

NORAH. That's enough! It's not her fault.

DAVID. I know it's not her fault! But if she didn't look like that, do you think this shit would have happened?

LEAH. Shut up, David!

DAVID. Don't tell me to shut up. Nobody can tell me to shut up, especially you!

(to NORAH) What do you think went on in your son's head when he saw that?

(to WAHIDA) Either you have no self-awareness or you're just a slut. Or both. I don't know. Eitan is a simple boy who wants a simple life. Why did you have to appear and fuck all that up? Can't you see that you're too much for him? Men must flock around you, all you have to do is snap your fingers and you can have any man you want, so why him? Why didn't you leave him alone?

WAHIDA. If I were Jewish, would you still say I'm too beautiful for Eitan?

DAVID. But you're not Jewish! That's the point! Don't you see what's going on outside? Can't you see who's shooting at who and who's killing who? You're a Muslim—you're an Arab, aren't you? Doesn't it feel strange to be here? Surrounded by us? Don't you feel like you're on the wrong side? Doesn't it bother your parents that you're in love with a boy named Eitan Zimmerman?

WAHIDA. My parents are dead, Mr. Zimmerman.

DAVID. Lucky for you! I'm sorry, but right now, I don't give a damn. It's my son lying in there, not you! So I'm sorry about your parents, but I don't give a damn.

WAHIDA. Don't apologize, I don't need pity, which is more than can be said about you. Arab or not, Muslim or not, thinking that it was my looks that seduced your son says more about your opinion of your son and the way you see me than it does about my relationship with Eitan. But I'm used to being seen that way. You should know that if Eitan came to this country and is lying in that room next door, it was for you! Because of his love for you! Because what he wants most is to protect *you*!

DAVID. Protect *me*? Protect me from what?

WAHIDA. I don't know. Ask your wife. Ask your mother. Ask your father. Since when does a man like you hope that an Arab woman like me could give him the answers to life's mysteries?

DAVID's mobile rings. He answers.

DAVID. Papa? Where are you? / You're here?! / On the eighth floor. Where? / Don't move. I'll be right there. Don't move!

He hangs up.

He got lost in the hospital. I'm going to get him.

DAVID exits.

NORAH. You should leave. Go home to your friends and forget this nightmare before it shatters you.

WAHIDA. I'm already shattered. We are all shattered!

She exits.

NORAH. If they close down the airport, is there any other way out?

LEAH. There's Lebanon in the north. Impossible. You can forget about Syria. There's Egypt in the south, but they don't really like us. That leaves Jordan, but after the attack on the bridge, you're better off with the other three. If not, there's always hell.

NORAH. We absolutely have to get out of here.

LEAH. Yes. We all want to escape. But now we have to face it.

NORAH. No. We don't have to face anything. For years everyone has avoided everyone. You never tried to see us, we never tried to see you. We never so much as mentioned your name. You weren't dead, you simply didn't exist. This meeting is an accident. A mistake. It never took place. So we won't face anything. We'll just keep our mouths shut, say nothing. Yes, I know. But David doesn't need to know about any of this. We'll just carry on. Like before. Carry on.

LEAH. Too late. Much too late. I can't keep my mouth shut anymore.

NORAH. Leah, I beg you, on bended knee, I beg you.

LEAH. No, Norah, I no longer have the strength.

NORAH. But you have the heartlessness. Leah, listen to me, please. Truth is not a game. It's frightful, worse than justice, worse than everything. Not to be toyed with. Believe me. Sometimes I see it in my patients' lives . . . it can take six, ten years before they're capable of hearing the truth. There is a right time for lies and a wrong time for truth.

LEAH. Too late! You have your son next door, alive, out of danger, and when he wakes up, you'll be able to hug him, scold him, you'll be able to argue with him, and then make up with him afterwards and hug him again! But I've been waiting for fifty years. I'm full of strangled tenderness, scorched affection. I can no longer repair the cracks, everything is leaking. A mother's heart is a strange thing, isn't it, Norah? We think we no longer have a heart, that it's finally turned to stone. We strut and boast. Look, I'm a heartless woman, and the minute I saw him enter the room, everything collapsed, all the stone crumbled and I saw that nothing had changed since those days long ago when he came to cry in my arms. What do you think happened when I saw the two of you walk in here? The heart I thought I no longer had got caught in my throat.

NORAH. Remain heartless, Leah, as heartless as possible. If you still love him, let him hate you even more, so he'll want to leave and never want to see you again.

LEAH. I'm too old for heartlessness, or for forgiveness or anything else. The knife stuck in the wound has to be removed. Of the three of us, who is the closest to death? Do you know what happens then? You're obsessed with the looks you never received. Suddenly you realize you want to be seen differently by those you hate and who hate you. You come home from doing your shopping, you sit down in your empty house and you wonder who you did that shopping for, and sometimes, just for fun, you set the table for two and you have a conversation with the child you no longer have, the child you sent away with the harshest words, and in the course of the same meal he is ten years old and you're scolding him because he tore his clothes, he's seventeen and you're consoling him because someone broke his heart, he's twenty-eight and you're giving him advice about his work, he's thirty-five and you're hugging him because he's just told you you're going to be grandmother—all that in the space of one meal that lasted fifteen minutes, alone in your empty house, and when you meant to laugh, you start to cry and you stand up, you do the dishes, you wash your plate and you wash the child's clean plate too and you wipe the counter until it shines. Do you understand? So don't ask me to go on being heartless, not towards him. If this angel from heaven hadn't come knocking at my door, I might have been able, but you can't refuse anything to an angel, so I'm sorry, but I want him to look at me just once and see me the way I've dreamt of being seen, and I'll get that look. He'll get down on his knees, he'll beg me to forgive him for speaking to me the way he did, and I'll get that look, I will.

NORAH. You'll never get it. David sees nothing, hears nothing of what others feel for him. Good or bad. His feelings are all that matter. David believes he's right about everything, not out of pride but out of totality. And that's why we love him. He's a monster! A marvellous, unbearable monster, and like all monsters . . . if he falls apart, he'll take everything with him. Leave that knife in your wound, because I'm the who lives with him, who shares his bed every day, and I couldn't bear the hemorrhaging. It doesn't matter who fathered David. David is Etgar's son. Period.

ETGAR enters, accompanied by a MALE NURSE.

ETGAR. At last! What a labyrinth of stretchers and sick beds!

NORAH. Did you see David?

ETGAR. Isn't he here?

NORAH. He left to find you. Sit down. He'll be back.

ETGAR. You've been crying, dear, what's wrong? Eitan!

NORAH. He's alive, don't worry.

ETGAR. Ah, thank you! Thank you! He's alive. Justice exists! I was so worried, just waiting for more news! Can I see him, God's angel?

NORAH. He's still unconscious, but you can see him. Just rest a bit. You recognize Leah?

ETGAR. Leah?! David must be waiting for me downstairs. I'll go see, otherwise he'll get mad again.

NORAH. Stay here. Sit down. I'll go find him.

WAHIDA enters. ETGAR sits down. NORAH exits.

15. Hell

ETGAR turns to WAHIDA.

ETGAR. What a trip. We left Berlin two hours late and they checked our passports three times upon arrival. Once in the cabin, then when we left the plane and then at customs. You can't imagine, no barriers, no separate lines, a mob. Two hours to get through. And I have an Israeli passport. The others are still there. If you had seen us, so many people, at least ten planes, it was so crowded. There was one man beside me, my age, we looked at each other and he said: "Are they taking us to the ovens or what?" We laughed. You just have to stick me in the middle of a crowd that can hardly move and I'm back in hell.

WAHIDA. Sorry, I don't speak German. There's something I need to tell you, while David and Norah aren't here: if you want Eitan to wake up, you have to tell him his father's story. I apologize for being so brutal, but if you want him to heal, you have to tell him the truth. Tell him the truth he has come to find.

ETGAR. But who are you?

WAHIDA. I am the woman who loves Eitan . . . When he wakes up, tell him not to come looking for me. I'll come back. Tell him I've identified the real issues in my thesis and now I have to resolve them. Tell him that I love him and that I want him to delve deep into his abyss and I'll try to delve deep into mine.

LEAH. Just promise me you will stay alive, and most of all, promise you will stop asking for permission.

WAHIDA. Okay, you old witch. I've learned my lesson and I'll follow your advice. I'm going to change my jeans and I'm off to find some big dicks to suck. Goodbye, sir.

WAHIDA exits.

LEAH. It's caught up with us, Etgar.

ETGAR. Give me time to catch my breath.

LEAH. You've had thirty-five years to catch your breath.

ETGAR. Yes. You always got what you wanted.

LEAH. Everything. Except the child's love. Peace of mind. My conscience. What you stole from me. Come now. We're going to pay our debts.

They enter EITAN's room. Sit down at his bedside. After a long silence, and much muttering, they begin to talk to EITAN. The day goes by, planes cross the sky and words are spoken, his, then hers, until day's end and they have to leave. No reconciliation between them. The words were given as facts.

16. The abyss of time

Evening. EITAN's room. An EMPLOYEE is washing the floor. The machines are humming. The encephalogram lights up, the cardio signals accelerate. EITAN regains consciousness. He sits up. EDEN enters. She is dressed in her military uniform and armed.

EITAN. Wahida?

EDEN. No . . .

EITAN. Where is Wahida?

EDEN. I've looked everywhere for her. I stopped by her hotel, no luck, and they've cordoned off the whole neighbourhood.

EITAN. Where are we? . . .

EDEN. Jerusalem. A hospital. You slept for four days.

EITAN. In one village, there were people . . . I had to clear the houses, and in a cupboard, there was a child.

EDEN. You hallucinated my night. That's all I did for two days: enter, evacuate, set fire.

EITAN. There were lots of people . . .

EDEN. On the bridge? Yes . . . do you remember?

EITAN. A gasp. A noise . . .

EDEN. An explosion.

EITAN. Everything is dark.

EDEN. You just woke up. Your vision will come back slowly.

EITAN. Wahida . . . where is she?

EDEN. I'm going to look for her. I'll find her. Tell her you are awake. My name is Eden.

EITAN. I'll come with you.

EDEN. You can hardly move.

EITAN. The Promised Land, supposedly. Quite the promise.

EDEN. The promise is never what we think.

EITAN. I came here to discover the truth about my father, as if I believed truth could be found in the origins of anything. Forty-six chromosomes. That's what I always preached, and I didn't believe it myself.

EDEN. Now you have to see it through.

EITAN. No. My father has to be spared. Just find Wahida and forget my father.

EDEN. Do you think that will satisfy Wahida? That she'll go on loving you in a simple, normal life, as if none of this had happened?

EITAN. It will shatter everything.

EDEN. Who cares?! Let it shatter us all, as long as what we love is spared. Eitan, listen to me: Wahida, you and I, and everyone who died in the night, we are all the impossible reflection of a dream assassinated ages ago. Beyond reconciliation. Too much land stolen, too many children killed, too many buses bombed, too many rapes and murders. How can we forget what they do to us and what we do to them? So we ignore them! And when we have to attack them, we attack, and when we have to defend ourselves, we defend. We count our dead without counting theirs and when their dead are more numerous than ours, we celebrate victory and joy and we go back to our seashore and they go back to theirs. That's war. A war that will last another thousand years. It's a graveyard and we can't escape it because we are all grieving the same lost dream that has never been properly mourned. The dream of living together, between the sky and the sea, of sitting down at the same table and inviting the gods to celebrate Eitan and Wahida's wedding, before building a common city with gates always open to both horizons. That dream is dead and buried, but we have to revive it, so we no longer tremble when we face each other, or when the skin of one touches the skin of the other. That's why, no matter how desperate, even if there's no hope of winning, we have to force those who remain silent to speak. We have to lance the abscess of history! Go find your father, shed light on his story whatever it is, die if you must, tear the fabric of your life apart, destroy everything that shaped your sanity and Wahida will be able to go on loving you, not because you dared disobey your blood, your father, but because you and she believed in the same dream. Nothing else makes sense, Eitan, nothing, except perhaps the invisible birds of chance who come and go and drive us into each other's arms for reasons we cannot grasp. But we cannot approach those birds or cage them. We have to let them fly free in the light of our lives that pass faster than the shooting stars we pin our wishes on, before disappearing in the dark night of memory. Everything else is up to us, Eitan. Everything is up to us.

Planes fly overhead.

III
BIRD OF MISFORTUNE

17. Promise

LEAH turns on the TELEVISION.

TELEVISION. Good evening, ladies and gentlemen. Scenes of horror in two Palestinian refugee camps yesterday in Lebanon.

LEAH. Etgar! Etgar!

ETGAR. What? What's the matter?

TELEVISION. The images we will be broadcasting today are unbearable, but you have the right to see them because they concern our presence in Lebanon as part of Operation Peace for Galilee. Yesterday, September 18, 1982, west of Beirut, just one week after the assassination of Lebanese president Bashir Gemayel, Lebanese Christian militias entered the Palestinian camps of Sabra and

Shatila, where access is controlled by Tsahal, and they proceeded to massacre thousands of Palestinian civilians. We have captured the horror. Look at the image of this woman holding her son's body. How did the so-called Christian militias manage to enter the camps without the authorization of our army, who control all access? This is the question the Knesset will ask our generals today.

LEAH. I'm going to the school to get David. I'm going to tell him . . .

ETGAR. What?

LEAH. Everything. I'm going to tell him everything.

ETGAR. Not like this, Leah.

LEAH. How else? We have to stop stealing his life from him!

ETGAR. Think twice, Leah.

LEAH. Seeing that, there's no thinking twice. On the contrary. I'm going to tell him everything.

ETGAR. But what are you going to tell him? You're going to tell him about the massacres? Are you going to tell him you've been lying to him forever, but seeing the bloodshed today you feel obliged to reveal the truth? Do you think seeing the images of piles of bodies is going to help him accept who he is? What do you expect him to do with that?

LEAH. So what do we do then? Nothing? Take a vacation? Or buy a new TV? Do you remember our pact? We'll keep him until we find his mother, his father. The truth is we never really tried because we didn't want to find them. What do we do now?

ETGAR. We protect him!

LEAH. No, Etgar, no! We're not protecting him. We're protecting ourselves, because neither one of us could survive his disappearance, his departure. We couldn't survive if someone came to claim him and took him away from us. We wouldn't survive.

ETGAR. He is our son. We raised him, educated him and we love him. He comes home at night and he's happy. He loves you, he loves me. And he loves you more than he loves me! What matters most, Leah?

LEAH. But what do I do now, if I still can't open my heart to him, fall on my knees and ask him to forgive me? What do I do? It's already unbearable with what's happening here, with the peace you promised me nowhere in sight, but if what just happened is true, if these massacres took place the way they say, if we Israelis played a role in the screams of that woman whose face they just showed us while she's struggling to carry her son's dead body, how can I possibly go on talking to him? How can I listen to him, when I know what I know and that he doesn't know?

ETGAR. David is fifteen years old. If you tell him the truth today because of this atrocious massacre, you will destroy him.

LEAH. Then I'm going to destroy us, Etgar. I'm going to destroy us. You will take him and leave. You'll send him far away from here. From me. I don't want to see him anymore.

ETGAR. Leah . . .

18. The speed of truth

Still in LEAH's apartment, thirty-five years later. DAVID, EITAN, NORAH and ETGAR enter with their luggage and their coats. LEAH leads EITAN to an armchair facing the window.

LEAH. Sit there. You can see the open sky, a real luxury in this city. You can all leave your bags there.

DAVID and NORAH put their luggage down.

What would you like to drink? I only have water. Anyone want something to drink?

NORAH. Water.

LEAH leaves the room.

We never should have come here. We should have left our luggage at the hotel, kept the room and paid the extra night.

DAVID. Eitan wanted to visit her before leaving.

NORAH. Yes, but you shouldn't have come with us and put yourself through this.

NORAH's mobile rings. She answers.

Hello? / What's the matter, Franz? I really can't talk now. / Yes, I read it. What's happening? / I understand that several Christian organizations have demanded that you prove the sperm is yours. /

You should call your lawyer, Franz, not your psychiatrist. / That's not the problem. / Your work sells based on the performative aspect of ejaculation, and the quantity ejaculated is impressive — you don't paint miniatures, do you? / So should it turn out that part of the sperm you used to execute your paintings was not yours, you could lose your reputation and you would pay the price dearly. / You can lie to me, Franz, but not to the law. / So accept doing the swabs. / On the contrary, this will be the first time in art history that a work of art will be submitted to a genetic test to prove the artist's paternity. / On the contrary, it's very postmodern, very contemporary, very German. / Settle the legal question and we'll deal with your trauma afterwards. / Today. / Call me tomorrow. / I'll try to fit you in between appointments.

She ends the call.

To each his own problems, right?

ETGAR. She's changed everything. I don't recognize a thing.

DAVID. Why? You've been here before?

ETGAR. This is the apartment where you grew up! Didn't you recognize the entrance to the building? The kitchen was there. The staircase to your bedroom was over there. This was the living room and the window was there, I think. And your blue piano was over there. Don't you remember? She tore it all apart.

LEAH returns with glasses of water on a tray.

LEAH. We have to talk. Sit down.

DAVID. I'll be late.

LEAH. So you'll be late.

DAVID. If I miss this practice, I won't be able to participate in next month's competition.

LEAH. You won't be participating anyway.

DAVID. Why?

LEAH. Your father and I are going to separate.

DAVID. I don't understand.

LEAH. We're getting a divorce.

DAVID. What's going to happen?

LEAH. I'll keep the house.

DAVID. And Papa?

LEAH. He's found a position in Berlin.

DAVID. Berlin? He's going back to Berlin?

LEAH. Yes. Apparently now the Germans love the Jews.

DAVID. How does that affect the competition?

LEAH. You're going with your father. He has custody.

DAVID. Is this a joke?

LEAH. You'll learn German and you'll fit in.

DAVID. I don't want to go to Berlin!

LEAH. There's nothing to keep you here.

DAVID. There's you! I want to stay with you. I don't want to go with him!

LEAH. We'll celebrate your birthday next week and you'll leave right after that.

DAVID. What about you? Don't you want to keep me with you?

LEAH. No.

DAVID. Why?

LEAH. I can't.

DAVID. Why?

LEAH. I don't love you enough, not the way I should. Don't cry, it doesn't help . . . The freezer's broken so I don't have any ice cubes.

NORAH. When the weather's hot, it's better not to have ice-cold drinks.

DAVID. So, I'm off.

ETGAR. You've got time.

DAVID. With the latest attacks, it will take hours to reach the Wall and I want time for my prayers. I'll come back to pick you up in a taxi and we'll go straight to the airport.

ETGAR. We'll wait for you downstairs. You won't have to come back up.

DAVID. There's the luggage.

LEAH. I won't be here, if that's what you're worried about. You can slam the door behind you.

DAVID. Fine. That'll be the second time we take our bags out of this house. So. What should I say: "goodbye" or "see you next time"?

LEAH. Better not to say anything.

DAVID. Once again, you've managed to ruin everything.

ETGAR. Wait for me there. I'll meet you. We'll have a bite to eat and come back for Norah and Eitan.

DAVID. If you want.

DAVID exits.

ETGAR. Sit down, my boy. Everything's fine, don't worry, it will all work out, won't it, my boy? Your father's gone, we can breathe.

NORAH. You should leave with him. It's unbearable here for you too.

ETGAR. Don't worry, everything will be fine. There's no point in worrying anyway, because nothing ever turns out the way we want. Does it? Everything's out of control and no one can foresee anything. Before, farmers raised farmers, kings, kings, workers, workers, you were born into a world and you didn't leave it until you left in a coffin. But now . . . the man who says "goodbye" ends up coming back, and the one who says "see you next time" is never seen again. It took the destruction of my world for a boat to bring me here. I had never seen an olive tree in my life, never eaten a fig! All I knew was fields of beets. And I arrived here. I can still remember. I wasn't even ten years old and I saw the sun, I saw the sea and all this light, and I was convinced my travels were over. Here, Israel, here, the world, here, the centre. I was the last in a line of birds without a branch, without a port, me, with nothing, the little survivor who saw my brother being hacked to pieces to feed the dogs whose slobbering I can still hear . . . I was stepping foot on terra firma, carrying the exile and the suffering of all my ancestors on my shoulders. I was arriving for them! Well, let me tell you something: if God exists, he must have been laughing because, in no time at all, I was packing my bags to return with your father to that cursed land, promising I would never set foot here again. And I believed in that promise. And now. Where am I? From where am I speaking to you? Funny, isn't it?

EITAN. Why can I no longer look my father in the eye?

Silence.

I'm speaking to you, both of you.

ETGAR. What do you mean?

EITAN. Okay. You are not my father's father. And you did not carry him in your womb. You found him.

NORAH. What are you talking about?

EITAN. I want to know if I really understood what I understood, and really heard what I heard.

NORAH. You were in a coma. It's normal. You're suffering from a kind of post-traumatic distortion and everything is all mixed up, the terrorist attack, this country, the war—all that has produced hallucinations: you think you heard something, you think you understood, but it's a nightmare, just a nightmare.

LEAH. You did hear and you understood very well. Your grandfather and I spent an evening at your bedside telling you that nightmare.

NORAH. What?

LEAH. Two days later he opened his eyes.

NORAH. Why did you do that?! What did you tell him?!

LEAH. Everything.

NORAH. What do you mean, everything?!

EITAN. Words are surfacing that I couldn't have invented. If these words are true . . . I don't want to betray my father, too, adding betrayal to betrayal, lies to lies.

ETGAR. It wasn't a betrayal, Eitan.

EITAN. What was it then? What's the right word for that?

ETGAR. We saved him. I saved him.

EITAN. I'm going to find him, I'm going to tell him, I'm going to tell him everything.

LEAH. It's not up to you to do that.

EITAN. It's up to who then? The two of you? You didn't do it. You didn't do it, Leah.

LEAH. Not like that.

EITAN. How else? He's my father. Is he your son? Or yours? No! So how else?

NORAH. Eitan!

EITAN. Let go of me. Let me go!

LEAH. Wait, Eitan. Listen to me! Not here! Not now! My angel, my dearest, my light, my joy, listen to me and tell yourself one thing, one thing that you can't see, that you can't even imagine: the truth that you want to tell your father and the truth I also dreamed of giving him is nothing next to his love for you. Nothing else matters. Listen! If he had any idea of your love for him, the love you're expressing now, if he could witness it—he is so convinced you hate him—if he could see how you're defending him against us, he would fall face first on the ground. I know him. I know him as if I had borne him: he would say he was seeing God! That love, more than any truth, is enough to make him happy because what matters most to David is Eitan's love.

EITAN. What do I do now? How do I manage to talk to him again? Listen to him? What do I do now that I know what I know and that he doesn't know?

LEAH. That question has been torturing me for fifty years, but I am his mother, you are his son. You owe him nothing. You are free. You're twenty years old. Don't listen to anyone. Your friends are waiting for you. Wahida is waiting for you. The conversation with your father will happen.

NORAH. Do you know how I learned that I was Jewish? How suddenly I found out? I was fourteen years old and I was happy we were having chocolate for dessert. Chocolate was so rare in the East. The evening news was on Soviet television. As usual, my father turned up the volume. "The GDR solidarity committee is denouncing the massacre of Palestinian civilians in the refugee camps of Sabra and Shatila west of Beirut. The TASS news agency reports that this brutal massacre was perpetrated by the Israeli aggressors with the obvious consent of Western imperialism." Watching the series of images, my father says, after this massacre if we ever hear him remind us that we are Jewish, he will cut out his tongue. Why did you say that, Papa? Remind us of what? That we are Jewish? Get that out of your head, Norah, it's all over now! We are Jewish? Why didn't you ever tell me? What good would it have done to know that your whole family was reduced to ashes? What?! What?! What are you saying, Papa? You are a Communist. Eat your chocolate, brush your teeth and go to bed. I saw the camps, the piles of hair, the bars of soap, and I threw up the chocolate and I thought, Norah, your skin is Jewish, your hair is Jewish and you didn't know it, and you find out by accident because of a massacre in a city you don't know in a country you never heard of. Like the child the blast of the explosion doesn't reach and she stands there stunned, holding the torn-off hand of her dismembered mother, I stood there holding the hand of the Jewish girl I was and that I had never known. I felt that little girl's aloneness, left without a mother, without sisters, without a family, stunned by the explosion of that stupid sentence spoken by my father who had no idea of its violent effect on his children. It's not the truth that gouges Oedipus's eyes, but the speed at which he receives it. It's not the wall that kills the race-car driver, it's the speed at which he crashes into it. If you love your father, if you want to cure him, don't put him through what I went through. Not too fast. Slowly, cure slowly, console slowly. Throw nothing too fast at the wall of knowledge.

The doorbell rings. LEAH *answers and* EDEN *enters.*

EDEN. Leah Kimhi? Eden Amitai. The door was unlocked, I came in. Wahida sent me.

EITAN. Eden! What's going on? How is Wahida?!

EDEN. She wants to see you. I've come to get you.

EITAN. We're leaving today.

EDEN. I know, your flight is at five o'clock.

EITAN. I won't take it.

EDEN. She wants you to go home. I'll bring you back here and I'll accompany all of you to the airport. I'll get you through security. You won't miss your plane.

EITAN. I'm not saying goodbye to you, Leah. On the contrary. I will be back to see you, I promise.

LEAH. Don't promise anything. My heart is yours.

EITAN embraces LEAH. EITAN and EDEN exit.

NORAH. She's going to leave him. I know it.

LEAH. She has to defend herself.

NORAH. It will destroy him.

LEAH. This is what you wanted, isn't it? You should all be happy.

ETGAR. That's how it is, my dear. Let him live his life's story.

LEAH. Too bad you avoided yours when you escaped the gas chamber, it would've been good riddance. But it wasn't your story, only that of six million others.

ETGAR. It will all work out. Everything will be fine, everything will be fine.

LEAH. Of course, because everyone will leave, and nothing will be said, nothing will be known.

ETGAR. You never tried to understand me, Leah. I'm going to find David. I don't want to keep him waiting.

LEAH. That's right. Go talk philosophy with your son.

ETGAR. I was happy to see you again anyway.

LEAH. Not me. I hate you, Etgar.

ETGAR *exits.* LEAH *bursts into tears.*

19. Arab

Seashore. Sunlight and blue sky. WAHIDA *and* EITAN.

WAHIDA. I went to the other side of the wall. I wandered in the dust of Palestine and I felt I had come home. I slept in the homes of people I didn't know and when they asked me my father's name, I burst into tears. Never since his death had I heard my name pronounced so well. Wahida, Wahida, why are you crying? I am mourning my father's gentle presence. Perhaps it was to hear the song of his name that Wazzan went home. At night, it was war, dawn brought the burial of the dead, crying for the living, cleansing the sorrows, weeping and fear. No one wants to be consoled. Anger has to be kept alive, you have to hate the enemy.

EITAN. Am I the enemy?

WAHIDA. I don't want to hide anymore.

EITAN. Then come back, with me. Let's go home together.

WAHIDA. No. We can't pretend that nothing happened.

EITAN. I have the right to love you the way I want.

WAHIDA. That's not the point. Look! Nothing is the same! Someone pressed the reset button. Like after a rape. Do you expect me to get up and walk around as if nothing happened? Like you, I sincerely believed we could be indifferent to the world. But no, the truth is I have nothing in common with the girl I thought I was, that girl who her whole life long invented herself in the eyes of others and who landed here two weeks ago, the girl you love.

EITAN. Wahida. You are Wahida. That's you.

WAHIDA. No. That Wahida is an illusion. There is no Wahida, or maybe I play the role, but I am not Wahida because I don't know who Wahida is. The attack destroyed everything, and all the mirrors have shattered and what's left is as simple as it is unbearable: I am an Arab. Stupid, isn't it? Your father was right, Eitan. I never dared admit it to myself. I am an Arab and no one taught me how to be one. On the contrary, I was taught to find it disgusting and I vomited it out of me. All of it. I bleached my complexion, I *untanned* my skin, polished it smooth. My good fortune was my beauty that blinded everyone and I banked on that, pretty mouth, beautiful figure, big breasts, a nice ass, and no one could say, "Did you see the Arab," but, "Did you see the bitch." I reduced myself to being a hole, and in the America where I grew up, that free Western world, so open, where everything is there for the asking, that all-powerful, vast, enormous America, I preferred a thousand times over to be seen as a good lay rather than have them shout the word Arab at me, a thousand times better to be called a slut than an Arab. That is the truth about Wahida, Eitan. Ever since I was born, I was taught to scorn and to hate everything remotely Arab, except for the food, and that is what blew up in my face in the glaring sunshine of this war. What an idiot! I thought I had nothing to do with all this, the poverty of the Arabs, the ugliness, the fat, veiled bodies. I really believed it wasn't my culture, not part of my life. What an idiot! These are my relatives! My sisters, my brothers! All of Ramallah smells like my mother. How do you expect me to survive! I believed all this had nothing to do with me. That we had taken this trip for you, because you needed to know who your father was and who your father's father was. I thought I had just come to support you. Not for one minute did I think that coming here involved me. Maybe because in the mind of a poor girl like me, when something happens to the man, nothing can happen to the woman, what happens to the man is always more important than what happens to the woman. What happens to you will always be more important than what happens to me. Your research will be more important than mine, your life more painful than mine, your story more extraordinary than mine. Because you are a man and you are Jewish, and I am a woman and I am an Arab. And tell me, how can the poor history of the Arabs match the history of the Jews? I know this isn't how you think, that an idea like that never crossed your mind and that's why I love you, why you are the man of my life, but for you, being the centre is obvious, you don't think about it. Then we arrive here. And I see it. I am an Arab. I might be an intellectual who fled to the opposite end of the world, I might have changed languages, hold an American passport, I might have met you, a Jew, the enemy, I might not give a damn about religion or the rest of the world, that doesn't change a thing. That is what I am.

For the past three years, I've been working my ass off on a thesis meant to prove how dangerous it is to let the principle of identity dictate your life, how stupid it is to cling to your lost identity, as if that had nothing to do with me. That's all academic bullshit. Bullshit ideas! The reality is simple. *This* is what I am. I belong to *this*, and if I want to escape it, I have to start by taking a look at myself. There's one thing I failed to understand, or didn't want to understand about al-Wazzan, and that's his curiosity and his many ways of being Arab, and the way he always escaped disaster. I have a lot to learn in that way. He didn't conceal who he was. He chose to reveal himself so he could pursue his passion for the world. I no longer want to escape, even if it scares the shit out of me, even if everything tells me I should go back and forget all this, I don't want to. I don't want to go back with you, back to New York. It would make no sense. I have to face *this*. Not as a tourist or a theorist, but directly, now, sacrificing everything, here, in the thick of it, on the other side of the wall, in the middle of this war. Forgive me, Eitan. Forgive me, my love. Forgive me, but I needed you to wake up so I could leave you. I am leaving you. I say these words and I feel what it's like to blow yourself up in the middle of a crowd. I'm smashing everything, I'm smashing us, I'm dividing the earth and I'm walking away. It's selfish, but during this war my place is over there, on the other side of the wall. With the ones who will lose. I want to stand by my sisters. At least, those who called me their sister. *Ya ikhti.* I want to stand by my mothers. At least, those who called me their daughter. *Ya binti.* You see? I simply say those words in Arabic, and I tremble, a sign of everything I've lost.

Long pause.

EITAN. Look up. What do you see?

WAHIDA. Birds.

EITAN. Birds. So I can't hold you back. Birds fly back and forth from both sides of the wall. When they are over there, they are there, when they are here, they are here. Who could deny that? But there are quantum birds, here and there at the same time, born like us at the moment of the Big Bang, who always fly at noon between two tides. I promise you. I would be crazy to complain. Two years of happiness. For someone like me, what good luck! Ever since we walked down those stairs, every second spent together was a second gained because I was spending it with you, and even this second spent here, so bitter, here and now. With you I received everything as a gift, every caress, every kiss, but every day, I swear, I prepared myself for this moment when you would leave me. I awaited it the way we await death: one day it will happen. But there's no preparing for it, no way to hold on to anything, and I will swallow the entire Dead Sea when you stand up and walk away.

WAHIDA. We're separating, but that doesn't mean we're separating. We have to believe in our reunion, act like the heroes, Anne Hathaway and Matthew McConaughey, when their spaceship falls into the black hole. They love each other but they separate, although nothing can separate them, and they don't know if they'll see each other again. Our spaceship is falling into the black hole of this land and here we are, each carried off to an equation we will have to solve alone.

EDEN enters.

EDEN. I have to take you back now.

EITAN. What's going on?

EDEN. Three bombs just exploded at the Tel Aviv airport.

EITAN's cellphone rings.

EITAN. Papa. / Yes, I know, where are you? / I'll be right there.

He hangs up.

WAHIDA. What will happen now?

EDEN. Now no one will have pity on anyone, Wahida. If you want to go back to the other side of the wall, you have to leave now.

EITAN. Go with her. The spaceship is falling and everything is separating us. Anne Hathaway and Matthew McConaughey are reunited at the end of the film, even if the damn credits prevent us from seeing them embrace in the thrill of their reunion.

WAHIDA embraces EITAN. WAHIDA and EDEN exit. EITAN exits. Sirens.

20. Punishment

Coffee shop. DAVID and ETGAR. Television news broadcast in Hebrew. Turmoil. DAVID is on the phone.

DAVID. They've closed down the airport, Norah. There are no flights. There are no rooms available. / Also completely booked.

/ Did you check every hotel? / I don't care, I'd rather sleep in a dump than her house. / We're still at the coffee shop, waiting for Eitan, then we'll come to get you.

DAVID *ends the call.*

She can't find anything.

ETGAR. It will work out.

TELEVISION. The first detonation took place at 12:40 on the arrivals level, a half-hour after the arrival of the flight from Washington, and the other two explosions took place at 12:42 on the departures level. All three explosions were probably the work of suicide bombers. These events are reported to have taken thirty-six lives, but that number remains preliminary. Air traffic has been totally suspended and all access to the airport has been closed off. The prime minister has not yet issued a statement, but his office is urging all political parties and the media to exercise great caution. No group has claimed responsibility for the attack, and at this point, the perpetrators have not been identified.

DAVID. This is punishment. Our punishment. Our terror.

ETGAR. You couldn't have known. No one could have known.

DAVID. I'm not talking about the attack: I mean them. Palestinians, Arabs. They are our punishment. For the past seventy years, God has placed them in our lives to punish us.

ETGAR. Why would God want to punish us again?

DAVID. Only prophets can say, but prophets always raise their voices in the wilderness, and we remain ignorant of God's plan. But our ignorance doesn't make us innocent. We are not innocent. Future generations will understand our sins, just as we understand the sins of our ancestors.

ETGAR. Do you believe God would have created a people solely as our punishment?

DAVID. We will uproot them. I wouldn't want to be a Palestinian today. As a people they've become little more than animals. Beasts, packs, assassins. If there is a truth, it is that, and this carnage proves it. They live in packs, they reproduce in packs, pray in packs and Islam is their bone. They gnaw on it like dogs. They send their children to their death, they condemn their poets, they subjugate their women and some dare to compare us, saying that Jews and Arabs are both Semitic races. We are no more like them than birds are like fish. They are the descendants of backwards tribes that landed here in the wake of fire, rape and bloodshed, and today they dare lay claim to this land when they have stolen it from us. They dare present themselves as victims when they are the criminals. They exhibit the bodies of their children, the tears of their women, and accuse us of exterminating them. Curses on you, wretched Palestinians. They will dance in the streets of Ramallah tonight and celebrate their gruesome victories, but the punishment that will befall them has no name. The best thing about these attacks is that they put an end to the myth of two countries living side by side. Let's hope the number of casualties is so high it will fill us with rage. The coming days will be bloody and unjust but today blood and injustice are the only way to conquer this leprosy. This land is ours, we will remind them.

The Arabs have to be reminded of their origins. They have to be sent back to the Arabs. They came from the desert, they have to be sent back to the desert.

EITAN *appears.*

EITAN. I'm sorry. I had to take a thousand detours.

DAVID. The most urgent thing now is to find a hotel.

EITAN. They're evacuating all the holy sites, it's impossible to get around.

ETGAR. Did you see your girlfriend?

EITAN. Yes.

ETGAR. You can join her since we're stuck here.

EITAN. No.

ETGAR. Why? Did she manage to get out?

EITAN. There are a lot of casualties. At least a hundred dead.

DAVID's *cellphone rings. He answers and walks off to the side.*

DAVID. Norah? Did you find anything?

ETGAR. Everything will work out, son.

EITAN. Stop saying that every time something serious happens. My heart is reduced to ashes. So stop!

ETGAR. That's not what I meant, don't be angry.

EITAN. I wish you'd stop comparing everything that happens to a concentration camp, dammit! I'm going to pay for your apple juice.

    EITAN walks off. DAVID comes back.

DAVID. Norah found two rooms in a little hotel between Jerusalem and Tel Aviv. It will be perfect. Where's Eitan?

ETGAR. Gone to pay the bill.

DAVID. I think it's over between him and the girl. He'll get over it.

ETGAR. You can never know what will happen. During the war with the Arabs in 1967, they sent us to clear out a Palestinian village. It was a beautiful day, like today. We arrived and we began. House by house. After a few hours, I came to a house with a huge fig tree outside. I still remember that because we stopped and ate the fruit. Then I went inside, went down a little hallway and entered the room in the back. There was a cupboard. I heard a noise, like someone breathing, barely audible. I went over to the cupboard and opened the doors and saw a pile of empty shoeboxes. On the lowest shelf, there was one of those boxes used for boots, without a cover. I pulled it towards me and looked inside. A baby. You hear me? A baby wrapped in a keffiyeh. Do you remember the keffiyeh you found in my drawers one day and shocked, you asked me why I had that . . . well, that was the keffiyeh the baby was wrapped in. A little Palestinian fellah. I don't know how long I stayed there, kneeling, watching him sleep, that baby all alone in a village on fire. I took the box and went outside. I asked my commander what I should do, and he told me to take the child to the hospital along with the wounded. On our way, the baby opened his eyes. We looked at each other—he didn't cry, he wasn't scared, he stared at me and I stared at him. I was sitting in the back of the army truck with the box on my lap and my face leaning over his. "We will find your mother." I told him that in German. I started to cry. Why was I crying? I can't say but that short ride was all it took to change my life. At the hospital, it was absolute chaos, horrible. Stretchers everywhere with corpses and the wounded. The woman at the desk was dead tired, exhausted. She saw me, saw the baby and asked me if I'd come to register it, if I'd come for a parental certificate. I said yes. Maybe just to make it easy for her. She asked me for my ID card, I gave it to her. What name do you want to give him? David, I said. She wrote it down and gave me the papers.

DAVID. You gave the name David to a Palestinian child?

ETGAR. I gave him the name of a king.

DAVID. What became of him? Did you ever find his family?

ETGAR. You are that child. You.

DAVID. No. I'm talking about him. I guess I was born after him, since you gave me his name, but what about him? What did you do with him?

ETGAR. You were not born before or after. You are him. You are the baby I found in that shoebox, do you hear me?

DAVID. What?

ETGAR. That's right. You are Palestinian. You are what you hate. You are an Arab, you are not Jewish. That's how it is. Sometimes life is simpler than we think.

EITAN returns.

EITAN. Shall we go?

ETGAR. Yes. We better hurry or your mother will get worried.

TELEVISION. The Palestinian group Abou Hawssan has just claimed responsibility for the terrorist attack that struck the country today. The prime minister has announced that the army is prepared for action and that the air force has just destroyed three Syrian military sites near the city of Masyaf believed to be responsible for the fabrication of weapons destined for the Lebanese and Palestinian terrorist movements. He also declared that repeated offensives will be undertaken to eradicate the assassins who attacked us, and that no country can undermine Israel's determination to exercise our right to defend ourselves and to punish our enemies.

Sirens.

21. Afikomen

LEAH's house. Evening. Dinner table. Only ETGAR is eating.

LEAH. It'll be cold.

NORAH. I'm sorry. I can't even swallow my saliva.

ETGAR. I'd forgotten what a good cook you are.

NORAH. I don't understand, Etgar. I don't understand.

ETGAR. The words were there. I spoke them.

NORAH. It wasn't up to you. Everything isn't up to you.

ETGAR. Eitan was heartbroken and his father, instead of taking him in his arms, was excited about a hotel room.

EITAN. Who says I needed someone to take me in his arms?

ETGAR. We wanted to tell him anyway, we were constantly talking about it, now it's done. Me or someone else, what difference does it make?

NORAH. Can't you see you're humiliating him even more?

ETGAR. You're too sensitive, my dear.

NORAH. I'm not your dear!

LEAH. It's getting cold. Forget him.

NORAH. It's driving me crazy that he doesn't understand.

ETGAR. Because you understand?! You've been living with a man you don't love for twenty-five years and you're preaching to me? For twenty-five years you've insisted on creating an absurd family to prove to your father that he was wrong, and you think you can grasp the depths of my soul? You pretend to be a happy woman, a fulfilled woman. You're anorexic, you're depressed. You're incapable of defending your son. Your life is a disaster.

EITAN. Have you gone crazy?

ETGAR. No, my boy, I haven't. I've always been crazy. It was crazy to do what I did! Stealing a Palestinian child is craziness for any Israeli! You have to be nuts to steal an Arab child in 1967 when Arabs are the enemy. Why, in the middle of the war, would a soldier do something like that? Don't forget, I didn't find you cuddled in swaddling clothes. I found you in the stench of death, and that turned my life into a huge lie. Lies, lies and more lies! How do you think we managed to convince people that child was ours! We lied to our relatives, we lied to our friends, we lied to our country. We sacrificed everything for a Palestinian child, and we went on lying for over fifty years. "Why?" That question haunted me for years, prevented me from sleeping, until the most blessed of all days, the day of your birth, Eitan. I held you, a tiny thing just out of your mother's belly, and everything became clear. I stole David to give birth to Eitan!

EITAN. You insult my mother, you humiliate my father and then you dare say I owe you my life.

ETGAR. Yes, because it's true.

EITAN. I don't want this truth.

ETGAR. Truth isn't revealed through the number of chromosomes, my child. If it weren't for the craziness you're accusing me of, you wouldn't be here to accuse me.

EITAN. If my existence depends on you, then I'd rather lose it rather than owe a second of my happiness to you.

EITAN *picks up a knife and prepares to stab himself.*

DAVID. Eitan! Stop, Eitan, stop! None of that matters. It's love masquerading as unhappiness. Tear away its disguise and everything will be like it was before, everything will be revived.

EITAN. This is not what I wanted, Papa, I swear. I never wanted this.

DAVID. I know. I know, but I don't want you to fight because of me. My truth is unimportant, Eitan. It doesn't affect my love for each of you. On the contrary, it gives me courage for what was missing. I love you all.

NORAH. David . . .

DAVID. Don't worry about me. I am not alone in this trial. I have the crossing of the Red Sea and the desert, and the exile of my people. I have the destruction of my temple, the extinction of my friends and the sacred alliance with my God. The spiritual immensity of Israel. O everlasting Lord, I have all that is great and strong in You. If I think, "I am drowning in darkness," You will turn my night into light. Light or darkness, it is all the same to You. O everlasting Lord, You made me as I am, You wove me in the belly of my mother, and I praise You for making me such a marvellous creature. Is all that being taken from me? Nothing left to be given? No, Eitan, my son, my love, you will see, everything will go on as it was before and nothing will change. Norah, we will relive the mystery of our first kisses the day we met. Eat, please, everyone eat, and be blessed. It's as if I finally found it.

NORAH. Found what, David?

DAVID. Yes, it's there. It was always there, but I was looking elsewhere.

NORAH. What?

DAVID. What I was looking for and never found, what was breaking my heart and made me burst into tears so often, inconsolable, inconsolable, and finally I can see it, yes, it's there. I'm sorry, sorry . . . David, David, where is the hiding place, where is the *afikomen*, where is it, David, it's there, Mama, I found it, I found it, I found the *afikomen*, Mama, Mama, Mama, Mama, Mama, Mama.

DAVID falls.

LEAH. David! David!

LEAH and NORAH rush over to DAVID, who is unconscious.

IV
AMPHIBIAN BIRD

22. The spirit

Hospital. DOCTOR, NORAH, EITAN, LEAH.

DOCTOR. The CVA affected several areas of his brain. Three blood vessels burst simultaneously and brought on intracerebral hemorrhaging and lesions that destroyed most of the cells in the temporal lobe.

NORAH. Can he regain consciousness?

DOCTOR. Unfortunately, no. His brain is dead. Your husband won't come back. We are keeping him alive artificially.

EITAN. What's the point if he won't wake up?

DOCTOR. Organ donations.

Silence.

To be useable, organs have to be removed while the donor's heart is still beating.

NORAH. I don't believe it, I don't believe it.

DOCTOR. If we remove David's organs within the next few days, we can save four lives.

NORAH. But according to the Torah, to remove a man's organs while the heart is still beating is to commit murder. For my husband, failing to respect the restrictions of the Law is unthinkable.

DOCTOR. Sometimes saving lives is more important than respecting the letter of the Law.

LEAH. The truth is that he isn't Jewish.

NORAH. His heart is Jewish. His mind, his thoughts. His ID papers are Jewish. His whole life was Jewish. I can't believe it. Is there really nothing to be done?

DOCTOR. Talk to him. We should accompany the dying until the end.

EITAN. Can he hear?

DOCTOR. Neurologically, no. But who knows what goes on in his spirit.

EITAN. His spirit? I don't believe in spirits.

DOCTOR. It's what he believes that matters. What is his mother tongue?

NORAH. Hebrew.

LEAH. Arabic. His mother spoke Arabic.

NORAH. We don't speak Arabic.

DOCTOR. Find someone who does. There's no shortage of that around here.

The DOCTOR exits.

EITAN. He was robbed as a child. Robbed while he was alive. And even dead, he'll go on being robbed. Nothing is his.

EITAN exits.

23. The suitcase that never arrives

Hospital. Evening. WAHIDA, NORAH, LEAH.

LEAH. You came. Thank you. I didn't think I'd be so happy to see you again . . . My Wahida, sent from heaven. Eitan doesn't know you're here and he told me NOT to call you. He feels guilty about everything. A real Jew.

WAHIDA. Where is he?

LEAH. In Beer Hobba, the village where Etgar stole David. The little stone he'll want to place on his father's grave . . . he wants it to come from there.

WAHIDA. Why is the old witch crying?

LEAH. Her heart is broken, my angel. Everything is spinning, starting over and coming back like suitcases on the carousels in airports. And mine never arrived. I am still waiting. Like an idiot. This is the second time I've lost him, and I can't believe that he won't come back.

WAHIDA. Why did you call me? Tell me what you want me to do and I'll do it.

LEAH. Apparently, speaking Arabic to David might help him pass away peacefully. Eitan doesn't believe it for one minute, me neither, but what do I know . . .

WAHIDA. David hates me.

LEAH. No. That David no longer exists. Forget what he did to you, forget his name. David is the name we gave him, but his mother and father must have given him a name first. Do this for me. Who else could soothe the heart of the Palestinian lying in the room next door?

NORAH. You killed him. You killed him from the very beginning. We killed him.

24. Miscarriage

DAVID's room. ETGAR enters. NORAH exits, without glancing at him.

ETGAR. I don't believe it will do any good, but I have to talk to you. Eitan refuses to talk to me. Norah refuses to talk to me. Each one of us is locked away in a coma the others can't understand. I love you. Forgive me.

LEAH. Go away, Etgar. Go away for good.

ETGAR. I carried you in my belly for fifty years, but despite the love, something was not born. Immense hope, miscarried, still-born. We have to accept it.

He exits.

25. Amphibian bird

Still in DAVID's room. WAHIDA is sitting at DAVID's bedside.

WAHIDA. Aleph, bé, tâ, szâ, jîm, ha, khâ, dâl, dââl, rrâ, zây, sîn, shin, sâd, dââd, tââ, zââ, ainn, rain, fâ, kââf, kâf, lâm, mime, noûn, hah, wâw, ya. The alphabet that accompanied our birth, yours and mine, the alphabet of our ancestors whose extension we are. David, hear my voice. I am Wahida, daughter of Nawal, granddaughter of Nazira, great-granddaughter of Soulum, seller of brushwood in the High Atlas. Like you, I didn't know the skies of my birthplace, so to talk to you in our native tongue, I will talk to you about me, and to talk to you about me, I'll talk to you about a man dear to my heart.

WAZZAN *appears, in* DAVID'S *coma.*

DAVID. Who are you?

WAZZAN. Hasan, son of Muhammad the weigher.

DAVID. What are you doing here?

WAZZAN. I've been sent to you.

DAVID. Who sent you?

WAZZAN. Those who love you.

DAVID. How did you get in?

WAZZAN. Through the words of the woman talking to you.

DAVID. What does she want?

WAZZAN. To help you leave in peace.

DAVID. Why this language?

WAZZAN. It's the language of your mother.

DAVID. Why you? What do you have to do with me? How could you help me leave in peace?

WAZZAN. What you lived through, I lived through.

WAHIDA. Like you, Hasan al-Wazzan was kidnapped from his life. Like you he adopted the clothing of the stranger. Like you he changed religion.

WAZZAN. And like you, I carry the fragments of my twin brother, the man I would have been if none of that had happened.

WAHIDA. And like you, he became the friend of his enemies.

DAVID. You knew that you had been kidnapped. You were aware of that and aware of your conversion. You know the name your father gave you. You knew your father's name. Son of Muhammad the weigher. I was shattered. What is mine? What am I once I walk through this door? *I am Jewish* is false. *I am Arab* is false. *I am not Arab* is false. How can a man leave in peace when he discovers he is his own enemy?

WAZZAN. "Here I am" would be enough.

DAVID. No, what I wove all my life is too woven to be forgotten.

WAHIDA. David, I'm going to tell you the story my father used to tell me when I was a child. "A bird comes into this world."

WAZZAN. A bird comes into this world and in the course of his first flight he passes over the water of the sea. Light reveals the silvery-scaled fish below the surface. Moved by this unfamiliar beauty, the bird wants to meet them and falls towards the sea. But the other birds, his kin, catch him before he reaches the waves. "No!" says the wisest, "never decide to approach those creatures.

They are strangers to us in every way, and by joining them you would die just as they would die if they joined us. We are not meant to meet or to live together." The bird obeys and lives his life, but the sight of the sea always tugs at his heart. A taciturn bird, he stops singing. Until one day, stricken with a sorrow too heavy to bear, he thinks: rather than a long, unhappy life, give me one instant of ecstasy, and he folds his wings! In the blueness of the sky he falls towards the blueness of the sea and penetrates the surface. There he is, underwater, diving towards the abyss of light, and in the few moments left in his life, the bird opens his eyes. Myriads of multicoloured fish! The unsuspected satin of the depths! Unspeakable strange beauty. His heart is ablaze. The hour of his death is approaching but he doesn't care, he exists in his desire for the other, for what is different, and this desire is so absolute, so immense, so spiritual that in the very instant where death comes to seize him, gills grow in his neck! And he breathes! He breathes. The bird breathes. And breathing, flying-swimming, he moves among the fish with scales of jade, gold and pink, as fascinated with him as he is with them, and the bird greets them, saying, "Here I am! It's me! I am the amphibian bird arriving in your midst. I am one of you. I am one of you!"

DAVID. In your voice, I hear the language spoken by the mother I never knew. Your voice like a net cast on the sea to capture ancient fragments of me. We have to console those who are dying. Thank you. But as beautiful as your story is, it's a story to soothe the living. For the dying man, nothing is repaired. I would have liked to meet my son's children. And to walk again in the rain, to count the stars, enjoy moments of silence and speak quietly to things. I would have liked to grow old with my wife. I didn't realize how painful it is to regret the things we failed to reconcile. I feel as if now I know what I should have said and done.

WAZZAN. Not everything can be successful.

DAVID. You are right about that. Perhaps every life is based on a mistake. Even if I am not leaving in peace, may these last steps be mine.

DAVID dies.

26. A stone

DAVID's burial. EITAN steps forward, holding a stone.

EITAN. Papa. No rain to soothe your soul today, no blossoms falling from heaven, only the wind and a stone to place on your grave.

Papa, I raise the promised land to my mouth. I swallow its beauty and I invent a new language. Kaddish in my own way, I say *David*, your known name, but I cannot say your unknown name, which will always remain the most painful enigma for me.

Papa, I take that invisible name, the name of the child you once were and I hold it in the palm of my hand and I close my fist—I swear to you—I close my fist, forever, to protect its disappearance from disappearing.

Papa, I bow before your grave the way one bows before the immense sea. I gather up the golden particles of your life. Everything you were able to give me. I gather up the fragments of pain, everything you were able to tell me. And I place this stone on your gravestone. Let the wind rise, let the sea part and let the birds carry you away. Goodbye, my father, goodbye.

I will live my life and it will be what it will be, whole and ardent, but on the threshold of your death, I promise you: as long as your two names remain entwined in carnage, as long as their two languages battle in blood, I, Eitan, son of Norah and David, grandson of Leah and Etgar, the heir of two peoples who are tearing each other apart,
I will not be consoled,
I will not be consoled,
I will not be consoled,
I will not be consoled,
I will not be consoled.

EITAN *places the stone on* DAVID's *grave.*

The end.

Acknowledgements

Tous des oiseaux—the first show I have directed since my appointment as artistic director of Théâtre de la Colline—théâtre national—was written with the invaluable, vigilant and always generous advice of the great historian Natalie Zemon Davis, whose encounter and friendship have led me to imagine vast new realms of exploration. A director's first production is always an important event for a theatre company. It seals the bond between the new director and the company's permanent staff as it embodies the artistic vision that will guide the company in the years to come. For this reason, the decision to examine the Israeli-Palestinian conflict in this *first time* has a symbolic weight in my eyes, since it establishes the notion of the enemy, the Other, as an obsessive guideline. To make this symbol a reality, since theatre is always the work of a team, I want to name all the people who worked on this first show presented for the first time in the Maria-Casarès Hall at the Théâtre de la Colline on November 17, 2017. I want to name not only the cast and production crew but also the eighty-four people who make up the permanent tribe at La Colline, those people working in different departments whose constant or occasional involvement made this production possible through their concern, their commitment and their willingness to engage and defend this endeavour with joy and vigour.

W.M.

Mohamed Abdoune, Laurent Alaphilippe, Jalal Altawil, Lise Amiot, Arnaud Antolinos, Jean-François Assie, Dominique Audibert, José Babo, Inès Badra, Hélène Baldini, Cem Baran, Laurie Barrère, Kaddour Belhamici, Moussa Bellachen, Amine Bellahcen, Émile Bernard, Isidore Bertin, Marie Bey, Eli Bijaoui, Anne Boisson, Majid Boukhadda, Franck Bozzolo, Bernand Brie, Menty Camara, Sylvère Caton, Jules Chagachbanian, Éric Champoux, Mathias Chomel, Sarah Clément-Colas, Emmanuel Clolus, Sonia Constantin, Pierre Coslado, Pascal Delarue, Maude Deleglise, David Digonal, Anne Dorémus, Dorothée Duplan, David Durand-Camacho, Charlotte Farcet, Fouzia Fendi, Isabelle Flosi, Quentin Franchi, Mickaël Franki, Linda Gaboriau, Jérémie Galiana, Laurine Gandubert, Marie-Laure Garcia, Sophie Garnier, Jean-Michel Gay, Frédéric Gourdin, Chloé Gourgues, Nadia Guessoum, Stéphane Hochart, Isabelle Imbert, François Ismert, Anna Jacob, Raphaël-Lamaque Jean, Mélaie Joudiou, Thomas Jourden, Eleni Karaindrou, Cécile Kretschmar, Didier Kuhn, Samuel Le Borgne, Laurence Le Coz, Thierry Le Duff, Yann Leguern, Dimitri Lenin, Pascal Levesque, Anna-Lou Lindgren, Christelle Longequeue, Grégoire de Lorgeril, Yannick Loyzance, Olivier Mage, Jean-Frédéric Marcel, Bernard Martin, Guy Martinvalet, Laurent Matignon, Michel Maurer, Stefan McKenzie Main, Christian Ménauge, Uli Menke, Patricia Michel, Igor Minosa, Saeed Mirzaei, David Nahmany, Yuka Nakanishi, Valérie Nègre, Julien Nesme, Tuong-Vi Nguyen, Victor de Oliveira, Franklin Onyeagba, Marie-Julie Pagès, Fleur

Palazzeschi, Roxane Pastor-Lloret, Claudia Petagna, Thi Xuan Pham, Armande Pierre, Thierry Pilliot, Philippe Plancoulaine, Jean-Michel Platon, Jean-François Prost, Ludovic Rivalan, Leora Rivlin, Lise Roger-Jaffe, Judith Rosmair, Lucie Ruffet-Troussard, Paul Saintier, Darya Sheizaf, Gabriel Sierra, Rafael Tabor, Adeline Tahan, Fanély Thirion, Gilles Thomain, Emmanuelle Thomas, Florence Thomas, Harry Toi, Franck Tortay, Aurélie Toublanc, Stéphane Touche, Monia Triki, Marion Turrel, Raphael Weinstock, Souheila Yacoub, Vahram Yeghiazaryan, Natalie Zemon Davis.

Wajdi Mouawad (author of *Scorched*, *Tideline*, *Forests* and *Heavens*, among others) has established himself as a uniquely original player on the contemporary theatre scene. His plays have been translated into more than twenty languages and presented all over the world. In all his work, from his own plays and adaptations, from the productions he has directed to the novels he wrote, Wajdi Mouawad expresses the conviction that "art bears witness to human existence through the prism of beauty." He is the recipient of numerous awards and honours for his work. He is currently Artistic Director of Théâtre de la Colline—théâtre national in Paris.

Linda Gaboriau is a literary translator and dramaturg based in Montreal. She has specialized in translating drama and has translated more than 125 plays, including the works of some of Québec's most prominent playwrights. Her translations have been published and widely produced across Canada and abroad. Her work has garnered many awards, including the Governor General's Literary Award for Translation in 1996 and again in 2010 for *Forests*. She was named a Member of the Order of Canada in 2015.

First edition: May 2019. Second printing: October 2019.
Printed and bound in Canada by Imprimerie Gauvin, Gatineau

Cover art and design by Lino

PLAYWRIGHTS CANADA PRESS

202-269 Richmond St. W.
Toronto, ON
M5V 1X1

416.703.0013
info@playwrightscanada.com
www.playwrightscanada.com
@playcanpress

MIX
Paper from
responsible sources
FSC
www.fsc.org   FSC® C100212